WALKING ON
THE BRECON BEACONS

About the Authors

Andy Davies

Andy (left) lives with his wife and two sons near Marloes, Pembrokeshire where he works in marine nature conservation and writing and photographing for books. Landscape, wildlife, underwater and lifestyle photography are an important part of his life and he also pursues his own personal work creating limited edition prints of abstract and impressionistic wildlife images that can be seen at www.andydavies.info.

David Whittaker

David (right) has enjoyed the mountains of Britain all his life, walking and climbing in Wales, Scotland and the Lake District. He has also trekked and climbed in Nepal, Pakistan, Tibet, Ladakh, New Zealand, Equador and Patagonia.

He was head of a university unit of forensic dentistry, working here and abroad. He is now Emeritus Professor in the subject and in 2003 was appointed OBE for his work.

WALKING ON
THE BRECON BEACONS

by

Andrew Davies and David Whittaker

2 POLICE SQUARE, MILNTHORPE, CUMBRIA LA7 7PY
www.cicerone.co.uk

© Andrew Davies and David Whittaker 1995, 2010
Second edition 2009
ISBN: 978 1 85284 554 4
First edition 1995
ISBN 10: 1 85284 182 6
ISBN 13: 978 1 85284 182 9
Reprinted 1999

Printed by KHL Printing, Singapore

A catalogue record for this book is available from the British Library.
All photographs are by the authors unless otherwise stated.

DEDICATION

*To our families and friends who have shared this area with us
and especially to Tim, David and Jean.*

Acknowledgements

Special thanks are due to Jean Davies for transcribing many of the cassette tapes made while walking the routes, to David Davies for producing the finished diagrams and to Dorothy Whittaker for patient forbearance during long evening hours of writing.

We would like to thank the National Museum of Wales, publisher of *Studies in the Origin of the Scenery of Wales I – The River Scenery* at the Head of the Vale of Neath, for permitting us to adapt Dr FJ North's diagrams on the geological formation of the waterfalls and on Craig-y-Ddinas and Bwa Maen. We would like to express our gratitude to the Merthyr Tydfil and District Naturalists' Society, publisher of *The Historic Taf Valleys: Volume 2 – In the Brecon Beacons National Park* by John Perkins, Jack Evans and Mary Gillham, for their kind permission to adapt their diagram on the glacial activity in the head of Nant Crew. Thanks are due to Richard Preece, the Countryside Council for Wales Reserve Warden for the Brecon Beacons National Park National Nature Reserves, for his informative comments on the routes that pass through Craig Cerrig-gleisiad and Craig Cwm-du. Help was also received from the Brecon Beacons National Park Authority. Ben Evans, Project Manager, South Wales Coalfield Geo Heritage Network, gave expert assistance with geological information together with Professor Tony Ramsey.

Front cover: Waterfalls in the lower reaches of Cwm Llwch

CONTENTS

Advice to Readers

Readers are advised that whilst every effort is taken by the authors to ensure the accuracy of this guidebook when it goes to print, changes can occur during the lifetime of the edition which may affect the contents. Please check the Cicerone website (www.cicerone.co.uk) for any updates before planning your trip. It is also advisable to check locally on transport, accommodation, shops and so on. Even rights of way can be altered and paths can be eradicated by landslip, forest clearances or changes of ownership. We are always grateful for information about any discrepancies between a guidebook and the facts on the ground, sent by email to info@cicerone.co.uk or by post to Cicerone, 2 Police Square, Milnthorpe LA7 7PY. We must emphasise that you should not venture into the high peaks without the knowledge to use both map and compass or without the proper equipment.

Warning

Mountain walking can be a dangerous activity carrying a risk of personal injury or death. It should be undertaken only by those with a full understanding of the risks and with the training and experience to evaluate them. While every care and effort has been taken in the preparation of this guide, the user should be aware that conditions can be highly variable and can change quickly, materially affecting the seriousness of a mountain walk. Therefore, except for any liability which cannot be excluded by law, neither Cicerone nor the author accept liability for damage of any nature (including damage to property, personal injury or death) arising directly or indirectly from the information in this book.

To call out the Mountain Rescue, ring 999 or the international emergency number 112: this will connect you via any available network. Once connected to the emergency operator, ask for the police.

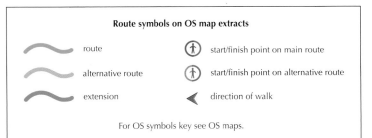

Route symbols on OS map extracts

route   start/finish point on main route

alternative route   start/finish point on alternative route

extension   direction of walk

For OS symbols key see OS maps.

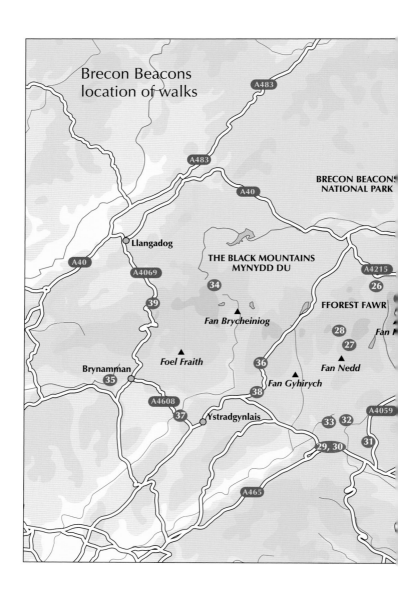

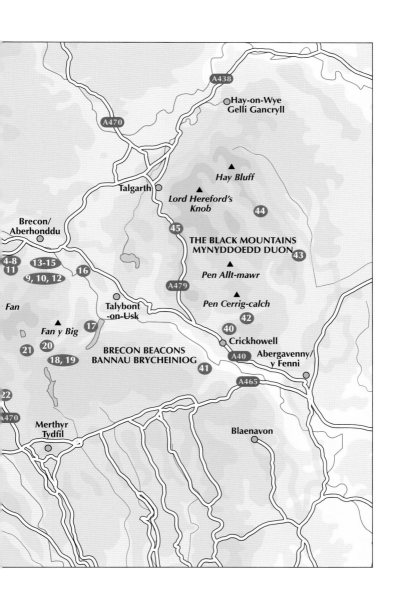

Western end of Craig y Cilau

INTRODUCTION

The Brecon Beacons from Cefn-Cantref farm

Situated in an unspoilt area of South Wales, just north of the former coal mining valleys, the Brecon Beacons National Park is a place of beautiful and diverse landscapes. One of three national parks in Wales, more than half of its 519 square miles are over 1000ft above sea level and it boasts a rich mixture of majestic valleys, dramatic waterfalls and high mountain peaks and ridges.

The routes in this guide avoid the less interesting, more popular routes that most people frequent, and take you to wooded gorges and upland valleys that even the locals may be unaware of. All the 45 routes are circular and avoid using stretches of road wherever possible. A striking feature of the park is the number of rich and varied walks that can be found in a relatively small area, so great distances do not have to be travelled by car to sample the multitude of different landscapes and varied terrain on offer.

The park falls naturally into four geographic areas. These are (from west to east): Mynydd Du (The Black Mountain), Fforest Fawr, Brecon Beacons and the Black Mountains (Y Mynyddoedd Duon). These all have different characters making the park unique in offering such varied walking experiences.

Mynydd Du really lives up to its name, having some of the remotest upland wilderness in England and Wales. This is the area to choose when

11

you really want to get away from it all. In contrast, Fforest Fawr (the Great Forest), a former royal hunting ground, has both friendly upland walks and deeply incised river gorges and waterfalls to rival any in the UK. The Brecon Beacons are the highest summits in the park, with Pen y Fan not quite making 'Munro' status, being just short of 3000ft. Although this area lacks the challenges of the narrow rocky ridges of the Lake District and Snowdonia, it does provide opportunities for a real mountain expedition in exciting winter conditions. Finally, the Black Mountains, on the English border, have a softer feel to them, without the coarse and rugged Welshness of Mynydd Du.

There is also a plethora of things to see and activities for visitors of all ages and tastes, making the park a great place for families to visit. Favourite attractions for children include Dan-yr-Ogof Show Caves in the Swansea Valley, Brecon Mountain Railway at Penderyn and Big Pit National Coal Museum near Blaenavon. Picturesque market towns on the edges of the park, such as Llandovery, Brecon, Crickhowell and Abergavenny, are also great places to explore.

GEOLOGY OF THE BRECON BEACONS

The rocks that shape the park belong to the Old Red Sandstone and were deposited some 395–345 million years ago in the Devonian period of geological time. Old Red Sandstone is a generic term which refers to a group of sedimentary rocks laid down by rivers flowing across coastal plains. Three distinct rock types, conglomerates, sands and muds, were formed from river gravels, sands and muds respectively.

South Wales lay south of the equator in latitudes which are typically occupied by deserts. Prior to this, much of Britain was affected by strong earth movements which caused uplift and sharp folding, resulting in a tract of upland (St George's Land) which probably extended from the Midlands through central and northern Wales and into Ireland.

Flash floods washed down red muds, sands and grits along ephemeral river channels, building an extensive river flood plain. To the south was the Devonian shoreline, approximately where the Bristol Channel is now, and the warm Devonian Sea where the first fish swam. Europe at this time was drifting northward and, when it crossed the equator, the semi-arid flood

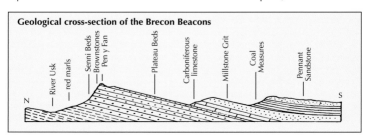

Geological cross-section of the Brecon Beacons

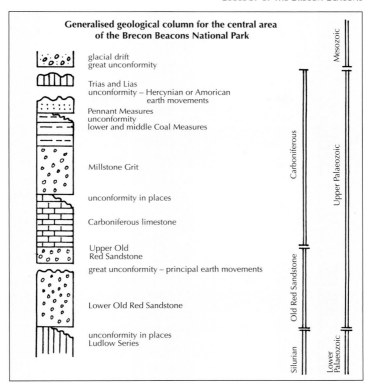

Generalised geological column for the central area of the Brecon Beacons National Park

- glacial drift
- great unconformity
- Trias and Lias
- unconformity – Hercynian or American earth movements
- Pennant Measures
- unconformity
- lower and middle Coal Measures
- Millstone Grit
- unconformity in places
- Carboniferous limestone
- Upper Old Red Sandstone
- great unconformity – principal earth movements
- Lower Old Red Sandstone
- unconformity in places
- Ludlow Series

Mesozoic

Carboniferous — Upper Palaeozoic

Old Red Sandstone

Silurian — Lower Palaeozoic

plains were gradually submerged beneath tropical Carboniferous seas.

The Old Red Sandstone in the Brecon Beacons can be split on geological grounds into Lower and Upper, the Middle being missing. The Lower Old Red Sandstone comprises a group of up to 850m of red marls followed by a group of sandstones divided into two formations – the Senni Beds, some 310m of dark green chloritic layers interbedded with red, and the Brownstones, 330m of very dark red and purple sandstones. The steep craggy slopes are formed from these regularly bedded Brownstones.

A secondary escarpment is well developed on the northern ridges of Cefn Cwm Llwch, Bryn Teg and Cefn Cyff where the ridge drops steeply from the main scarp, flattens between 540 and 600m and then drops again, the

13

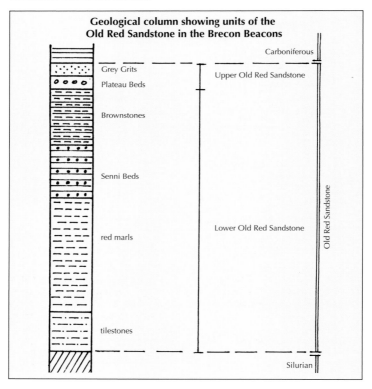

Geological column showing units of the Old Red Sandstone in the Brecon Beacons

Carboniferous

Grey Grits

Plateau Beds

Brownstones

Senni Beds

red marls

tilestones

Upper Old Red Sandstone

Lower Old Red Sandstone

Old Red Sandstone

Silurian

steeper slopes beneath this being cut in the Senni Beds which underlie the Brownstones.

The Upper Old Red Sandstone comprises three groups of rocks. The Plateau Beds are red quartzites and conglomerates up to 33m thick which unconformably overlie the Brownstones. The summits of Corn Du and Pen y Fan are capped by an iso-lated outlier of some 14m of overlying, massively bedded, Plateau Beds. The second group, the Grey Grits, are unfossiliferous sandstones and con-glomerates up to 200ft thick and these pass laterally eastwards into the Quartz Conglomerates which comprise red and brown sandstones, quartzites and coarse conglomerates. Further earth movements during the mid-Devonian period uplifted South Wales, resulting in renewed erosion, creating a distinct

Pen y Fan from the Cribyn face path

break in the geological record, and forming the distinctive ridges and valleys that walkers enjoy today.

Earth movements

Mountain building earth movements which took place at the base of the Old Red Sandstone and at the end of the Upper Palaeozoic have been named the Caledonian and Hercynian, respectively. Caledonian movements spanned a time interval of more than 100 million years, at least from latest Cambrian to post-Silurian, and were responsible for folding and faulting of rocks, resulting in geological structures aligned in a north-east–south-west direction. After these mid-Devonian movements died away, there was little mountain building until late Carboniferous times. At the end of the Coal Measures, the Brecon Beacons were on the southern flanks of a southward-moving continent which eventually collided with a northward-moving land mass to the south. Enormous compressive forces caused strong folding and faulting of Upper Palaeozoic rocks. The outstanding feature that resulted from these tectonic movements is the syncline of the South Wales coalfield and the regional southward tilt of the rocks of the Brecon Beacons originated as part of its northern limb. A major structure disrupts the northern rim of the coalfield and runs through the lower parts of the Waterfall Country. This is a complex fault system known as the Neath Disturbance which grew intermittently from Dinantian times, reaching its zenith in late-Carboniferous times.

Glacial origins of U-shaped valleys

The valleys were originally formed by streams cutting down through the Old Red Sandstone rocks, forming a V-shaped cross-section. For some two million years this area was in the grip of the Ice Age which ended about 10,000 years ago. Glacier ice carved out U-shaped valleys and towards the end of the Pleistocene, when climatic conditions were still sufficiently cold for significant quantities of snow to collect, many cwms were formed.

CHANGING WOODLAND

Trees started to recolonise the Brecon Beacons after the last Ice Age around 12,000 years ago. Arctic-alpine vegetation first established itself, and was then invaded by a scrubland of dwarf birch with some juniper. Taller birches and, to a lesser extent, Scots pine, followed.

The climate continued becoming warmer and drier and, around 9000 years ago, pine and birch remained on lower hill slopes but the upland was covered in hazel, with valleys full of damp oak woodland with lime and elm. Woodland grew at much higher altitudes than it does today, up to 600m, above which grew alpine grassland.

Climatic conditions then became even warmer and more humid allowing the formation of blanket peats 7000–5000 years ago. Alder, elm and oak thrived in damp valleys. Drier conditions returned, elm disappeared and beech made its first appearance. The climate started to decline again and has continued to do so to the present day.

Woodland flowers in Cwm Cumbeth

Sessile oak, ash and beech woodland developed in this period and still dominate the landscape today.

HUMAN IMPACT

The Brecon Beacons may appear to be a bleak and inhospitable place to live but prehistoric man is known to have settled here since Mesolithic times (Middle Stone Age c6000BC). The climate in Mesolithic, Neolithic (New Stone Age c3000–1800BC) and Bronze Age times (c1800–400BC) was much warmer and drier than today's and the mountains were covered in oak, birch, alder and lime woodland, with an understorey of hazel and willow.

Woodland glades would have contained grasses, heathers, species of rose and various flowers. Prehistoric man fed, clothed and housed himself by hunting and gathering, and, by about 2500BC, woodland clearance and mixed farming was practised. During the very dry summer of 1976 when the water level was extremely low, many scrapers, arrowheads and knife blades were found in the Upper Neuadd reservoir.

An improvement in Britain's climate from about 4500 years ago heralded the start of the Bronze Age and was associated with the spread of agriculture into the uplands at the expense of the wildwood. This change is suggested by a gradual decline in tree pollen and an increase in plantain pollen and bracken spores in peat cores taken locally. It is also known that cereals were cultivated in the Brecon Beacons area. The climate deteriorated again from about 3000 years ago and resulted in a retreat of farming from the uplands. Peat bogs spread across formerly productive farmland.

The Neolithic tradition of constructing stone circles was continued into Bronze Age times but now came the construction of large dry-stone cairn burial mounds on the summits of Mynydd Du and Fforest Fawr. Copper tools and other objects are recorded from at least 4500 years ago. The use of copper was followed shortly by bronze. However, stone tools continued to be made and used in Wales until about 3400 years ago.

A marked increase in deforestation took place during pre-Roman Iron Age times in order to create new grasslands, as sheep were an important part of the subsistence economy. Similar factors have controlled the appearance of the landscape from this time to the present day as farmers continue to make a living from the land.

BIRDLIFE

Merlins have declined due to loss of open heather moorland which has been decimated by conifer planting, agricultural improvement of moorland and overstocking of sheep. Their principal prey are meadow pipits which return to the moor in spring. Before this, merlins feed on small birds from surrounding lowlands, mainly chaffinches, tits and goldcrests. Ravens are numerous in the Brecon Beacons and are the great scavengers of the hills. Buzzards are also common and, together with ravens, are carrion feeders and find sheep carcasses whenever they can. Curlew can be found nesting among rushes of the higher streams but their camouflage is so good that you will rarely spot a sitting bird.

Dunlin nest among eroding peat hags and are at their most southerly breeding limit in the world. Golden plover are another true wader of mountain moorland and are again close to their southerly limit. You may disturb red and black grouse when walking across open moorland such as Waun Llysiog. Both species spend the winter on the mountains but the loss of bilberry, heather and cotton-grass moorland through conifer planting has resulted in their decline.

Bracken-covered valley slopes support dense populations of whinchat and also provide nesting areas for mallard, nightjar, stonechat, wren, tree pipit and yellowhammer. Damper patches may hide the dark-capped reed bunting. Skylarks are constant companions in spring and summer on grassy uplands, the air full of song as they fly above you. White rumped wheatear reside in drystone walls and bouldery scree. Look out for stonechat, linnets and yellowhammers in the gorse.

Woodland birds include blue tit, great tit, coal tit, pied flycatcher, nuthatch, redstart, tawny owl, green woodpecker, lesser-spotted woodpecker, great-spotted woodpecker, jay, wood pigeon, blackbird, treecreeper and wren. Warblers migrate in summer from southern climes to nest on the woodland floor.

The fields, wooded slopes and river of waterfall country provide a wide variety of habitats for numerous birds. Lapwing are commonly seen in the valleys together with redshank and snipe. Birds found associated with woodland and along the river bank include breeding dipper, grey wagtail, goosander, pied flycatcher, redstart, wood warbler, woodcock, buzzard and sparrowhawk.

GETTING TO AND STAYING IN THE NATIONAL PARK

The Brecon Beacons National Park is a day trip from Swansea, Cardiff, Bristol and the Midlands and an ideal short-break destination from London, only 200km (120 miles) away. There are excellent rail and motorway links with the rest of the UK and Cardiff International Airport is just over an hour from the park.

In summer, the Beacons Bus offers the opportunity to have a car-free day in the mountains on Sundays and Bank Holidays from May to September from many places in South Wales and Herefordshire.

If you want to stay over, the park has accommodation to suit all pockets, from grand country hotels to secluded campsites. More information on transport and accommodation can be found at Brecon Beacons Tourism (www. breconbeaconstourism.co.uk) along with suggestions on where to eat.

The Brecon Beacons National Park Authority manages the area and runs a number of visitor centres and a guided walk programme. Further information can be found on its website www. breconbeacons.org and in the comprehensive Visitor Guide.

A SOLITARY GUIDED WALK?

The inspiration for this guide came from a realisation that many walkers wish to know more of the countryside they come to enjoy and explore. One solution is to join one of the many guided walks organised by the Brecon Beacons National Park Authority. However, these are so popular that as many as a hundred people may join a single ramble. This is not only a logistical problem for the warden, but the sheer numbers destroy the wilderness quality of a walk in the countryside, with little chance of seeing undisturbed wildlife.

Another approach is a 'guided walk' with a difference – a walk guided by a book which gives you all the interesting facts that a walk with an expert would provide but still retains the magical wilderness feeling of an isolated mountain summit or the tranquillity of a river ramble. This guide aims to provide you with information on all aspects of the landscape, as if you were being accompanied and advised by several experts at the same time.

All the route descriptions are accompanied by a commentary that includes geomorphology, hydrology, geology, botany, zoology, ecology, ornithology, archaeology, local history, land-use and environmental issues. Designed to be used by all ages, the guide does not assume any previous mountain walking experience or countryside knowledge.

USING THIS GUIDE

This book is divided into seven geographic sections:

1. Brecon Beacons – North-Eastern Valleys and Ridges

2. Brecon Beacons – Eastern Valleys and Ridges

Sgwd Isaf Clun-gwyn

19

3 Brecon Beacons – South-Western Valleys and Ridges
4 Fforest Fawr
5 Waterfall Country
6 The Black Mountain/Mynydd Du (Western Brecon Beacons National Park)
7 The Black Mountains/Y Mynyddoedd Duon (Eastern Brecon Beacons National Park)

It is designed to be used in conjunction with the Brecon Beacons National Park Outdoor Leisure Maps (1:25,000): Western Area OL12, Central Area OL11 and Eastern Area OL13. The 45 routes described include low-level and high-level routes of varying lengths and degrees of difficulty to cater for different weather conditions and abilities. A fit mountain walker will not find any of the routes particularly strenuous. All the routes are circular, include as few roads as possible and explore little frequented areas.

For each route, the start point (including grid reference), distance, total ascent and map required are listed at the beginning of the route description. Routes are illustrated with extracts from 1:50,000 OS maps, with the main route marked in orange and any alternative routes marked in blue and extensions in green (alternative and extended routes are described at the end of the main route description). Features along the walk that appear on the map are highlighted in bold in the route description to help you follow your progress. The route descriptions are also accompanied by information boxes which are often cross-referenced by other route descriptions, using the title of the

box and the walk number (for example, see 'Cefn Cyff,' Walk 10).

The tables of Routes by Difficulty and Routes by Interest in Appendix 1 and Appendix 2 are provided to help you choose a walk suitable for the weather, the time you have available, your fitness level and your interests. Once you have chosen a suitable walk from the table, you will find it summarised in the introductory box at the beginning of each route. Some of the valleys, especially the northern ones, offer a multiplicity of routes and walks have been chosen using the ridges in a particular direction so as to present the best unfolding panorama. Valleys have been included to give shorter, less strenuous walks or as an alternative in bad weather when all but the most adventurous might eschew the high places.

How long will a route take?
A general rule of thumb for calculating the minimum time that a particular route might take to walk is to allow 1 hour for every 5km (3 miles) forward and an additional half hour for every 300 metres (1000ft) of ascent. This formula, known as Naismith's Rule, is based on a fit hiker walking on typical terrain under normal conditions. Once you have walked a few of the routes in this guide, you should have a clearer idea of how you need to tweak the rule to work for your own level of fitness.

Don't forget to add in time for rests, breaks for lunch and reading this book to arrive at a rough indication as to how long you'll be out on the hill.

Ling ▲

Bilberry ▼

Speckled wood butterfly ▲

Cowslip ▼

Bluebells ▼

Craig y Cilau from above Agen Allwed cave

1 NORTH-EASTERN VALLEYS AND RIDGES

WALK 1
Cwm Llwch and Cefn Cwm Llwch

Start	Llwynbedw, Cwm Llwch (SN006 246)
Map required	Central Map OL11
Distance	9.5km (6 miles)
Total ascent	620m (2035ft)

This is a fine route into the most westerly of the northern Beacons valleys and it progresses in a southerly direction into the valley head below the north face of Corn Du – the second highest peak in the range. The walk goes up the stream in the valley floor to a corrie lake. There are good waterfall views overshadowed by the looming bulk of Corn Du. It then works its way up the right (W) ridge and so up to the summit of Corn Du. From here it continues over to the summit of Pen y Fan (the highest peak in the Beacons) and returns to the start via the ridge, Cefn Cwm Llwch. An alternative shorter route returns to the start from the obelisk below Corn Du, dropping down Pen Milan ridge on the west of the valley. The final climb to the summits is steep, as is the upper part of the descent from Pen y Fan. Route finding is straightforward in good weather, but in mist or winter conditions ability to use compass and map is important. The walk requires a reasonable degree of fitness. Points of interest include glacial geomorphology, plants and birdlife, waterfalls and lake, good panoramic views and archaeological features.

Start at the end of the car park where there is a 'NO MOTORS' sign. The ford and the hillside on the left of the car park is your descent. Follow the track leading into the valley, lined with beech, hawthorn, mountain ash and hazel.

The woodland on the right contains the poorly preserved earthworks of an **Iron Age hill fort** which is marked on the map as a dotted oval and labelled 'Settlement'. This is a small enclosure with widely spaced ramparts. Its value as a hill fort is dubious as, although the land slopes away east to Nant Cwm Llwch, the land to the west and south rises gradually to the foot of Pen Milan.

The track soon comes to another ford across the same stream, **Nant Cwm Llwch**, with a wooden bridge on the left,

Notice the abundant ferns and mosses on the sloping roof of an outhouse on the northward facing end of the cottage.

through a second gate and then between wooded banks with fields on either side. From here there are good views into Cwm Llwch with waterfalls in the foreground and a backdrop dominated by Corn Du straight ahead and Pen y Fan on the left.

The track continues southwards between old stone walls and then detours around **Cwm-llwch Cottage**. ◄

Leave the cottage on your left and skirt around the right of the farmyard by crossing over two stiles. After about 100m there are good views into Cwm Llwch, with waterfalls in the foreground and a backdrop dominated by Corn Du straight ahead and Pen y Fan on the left.

The wide open track ahead takes a direct line up a spur of land with stream courses on either side. However, this line is of little interest and avoids the superb waterfalls glimpsed earlier. Descend instead to the left and walk along the fence, which soon reaches the stream. Here a small track crosses to the left bank, although either can be followed to the waterfalls.

This is a most interesting habitat as, after the birch woodland is left behind, the banks of the stream are lined with closely grazed grassy areas where there are many different species of wild flowers, such as lousewort (*Pedicularis sylvatica*), bird's-foot trefoil (*Lotus corniculatus*), red bartsia (*Bartsia odontites*) and eyebright (*Euphrasia sp*).

Notice that the valley slopes have a high density of hawthorn trees – a notable feature of Beacons valleys. For this reason, the number of bird species is more typically associated with woodland than an open valley. Keep a sharp lookout for tree pipit, green finch, redstart, wren, whinchat, yellowhammer and chaffinch. Even the great-spotted woodpecker has been recorded. Do not be surprised to see green woodpeckers often far from

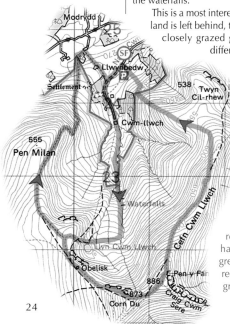

trees where they feed on ants. The falls and stream bed are good places to spot grey wagtail, heron and dipper. The valley is unusual in that there are two stream beds which have eroded the floor, leaving a raised spur of land in the centre (see 'Geology and geomorphology of Cwm Llwch,' Walk 3).

The hill fence crosses the stream ahead but there is a low-level stride over it just before the stream divides. The left branch of the stream is the more interesting and just ahead is an impressive **waterfall**. This can be climbed on the right arriving first at a small pool above the lower fall.

The falls are shaded by a mixture of hawthorn, black-thorn, ash, rowan, willow and silver birch. Most of the trees are young or have grown from previously fallen trunks. Luxuriant bryophytes and ferns thrive on damp and wet rock faces surrounding the fall. Ferns include the rare Wilson's filmy fern (*Hymenophyllum wilsonii*) and *Cystopteris fragilis*. Bryophytes include *Ulota crispa, Mnium undulatum, Hylocomium splendens, Atrichum undulatum, Neckera pumila, Fissidens taxifolius, Philanotis fontana, Hyocomium armorica, Frullania tamarisci* and several others. Several ungrazed tall herb ledges can be seen to the left and right of the fall. Interesting vascular plant species include valerian (*Valeriana officinalis*), wild angelica (*Angelica sylvestris*), meadow sweet (*Filipendula ulmaria*), *Alchemilla vulgaris*, wood avens (*Geum rivale*) and Welsh Poppy (*Mecanopsis cambrica*).

Climb up the right side of the upper fall or more easily up the hill on the right of the lower fall reaching a series of smaller waterfalls from where there are magnificent views of Corn Du. Surprisingly, the flat-topped summit of Corn Du at the head of valley falsely appears higher, from this viewpoint, than its neighbour, Pen y Fan, which is on the left. When the stream starts to break up into many smaller tributaries, leave the stream to the right, striking westwards to the corrie lake of **Llyn Cwm Llwch**.

Flushed areas at the head of the valley are extensively covered in soft rush (*Juncus effusus*). Llyn Cwm Llwch is a

Tommy Jones obelisk, Corn Du and Pen y Fan

good place to have a break and appreciate this special place (see 'Geology and geomorphology of Cwm Llwch'; 'Glacial origins of Llyn Cwm Llwch,' Walk 3).

Take the path which leads to the right (W) up the steep slope in a zigzag, climbing steeply to the lower end of the ridge of Craig Cwm Llwch, near to the **Tommy Jones Obelisk**, a useful landmark in poor visibility. The path has been severely eroded into a deep gully, firstly by the passage of feet which destroyed the protective turf, and now by a combination of walkers and water. It becomes a watercourse in heavy rain.

Looking back down to the left from the obelisk is a fine view of the hummocky mounds of glacial moraine that dam the lake of Llyn Cwm Llwch.

The obelisk is a memorial to **Tommy Jones**, aged five, who died here in 1900 of exhaustion. He was attempting to walk alone from Cwm Llwch Farm to an army encampment at Login. It now serves as a useful landmark in poor visibility by marking a rapid descent route from Cefn Cwm Llwch to the safety of the valley below ensuring that walkers today do not suffer the same fate. ◄

The alternative route to Pen Milan leaves from here.

Follow the ridge of Craig Cwm Llwch (SE) up the steep slope to the summit of **Corn Du**.

From Craig Cwm Llwch you may see many species of bird and see buzzard, carrion crow and raven wheeling overhead. Ravens nest nearby on the crags of Craig Cwm Sere. You will undoubtedly see or hear meadow pipit and skylark, the commonest birds over hill grasslands. If you are especially observant you may see ring ouzel as they breed in the vicinity of the crags. This area is near to the limit of their British range.

The final 10m or so to the summit of Corn Du involves scrambling up the Plateau Beds but a stepped path leading diagonally right will avoid further damage to these loose crags. An interesting path-cum-sheep track avoids this and cuts east across the northern face of Corn Du below the crumbling cliffs of Plateau Beds to the col leading to Pen y Fan (see 'Geology of the Brecon Beacons,' Introduction). The crags are covered in grazed purple moor grass heath (*Vaccinium*). Awnless sheep's fescue (*Festuca vivipara*) is the only plant species of interest. From the top of the stepped path cross left (E) to the summit of the crags overlooking Cwm Llwch.

Cefn Cwm Llwch and Llyn Cwm Llwch from Corn Du

From the cairn follow the crags (E) and descend into the col. The path swings around (ENE) and climbs along a broad track, well marked by cairns. The final one is of Bronze Age origin and leads to the trig point on the summit of **Pen y Fan**. Pen y Fan at 886m (2906ft) is the highest mountain in South Wales and just fails to achieve Munro status, a term given to summits over 3000ft. For a description of the mountain see 'Geology and geomorphology of Pen y Fan,' Walk 5).

PEN Y FAN VISTA

The summit of Pen y Fan is one of the finest vantage points in Wales. On an exceptionally clear day, Cadair Idris can just be distinguished to the north and Exmoor to the south. Fforest Fawr to the west possesses many interesting features and is a relatively unvisited part of the park. Almost due west are the cliffs of a beautiful glacial cwm, Craig Cerrig-gleisiad. To the south-west the plumes from the stacks of Port Talbot and Llandarcy can be seen on a clear day and in between these is the wide sweep of Swansea Bay which culminates in the west with the Mumbles Lighthouse.

Scramble carefully down the crags due north of the summit cairn and follow the ridge of Cefn Cwm Llwch for about 2km.

As you scramble down from the summit, look carefully at the upper surfaces of the near horizontal Plateau Beds for **ripple marks**. These are also present on the surfaces of rocks making up the summit. They were formed in exactly the same way as ripples are formed in the sandy beds of rivers today. Look back at the northeast face of Pen y Fan where in early spring you can see the brilliant colours of rare arctic-alpines (see 'Flora of the north-east face of Pen y Fan,' Walk 4).

Take a small path which leaves the main track and bears left (N) towards the pile of stones at the disused quarry of Cwar Mawr (SN018 236). From here descend west-north-west (292°) to the spur of Twyn y Dyfnant and down the steep slope to the hill fence, keeping to the right of the coniferous forestry.

Cross the fence through a gate (SN009 241) and follow the line of trees diagonally down the slope to the right. At the end of the tree line turn sharp left and drop down to the field below. An indistinct path leads directly down the field after 80m. Head for the junction of hedges to the left and continue down the slope to the ford across the stream (SN007 244) and back to the start of the walk.

Alternative route

From the obelisk turn north and follow the footpath which swings first right, left, then right again around the head of a side valley of Cwm Llwch, with steep slopes on the right. Just before the final spur of **Pen Milan**, the path changes into a broad green old quarry track. ▸

The route descends to the right diagonally across the valley side. This track has obviously seen heavy use in the past and, in fact, was used to transport Old Red Sandstone (see 'Geology' in the Introduction) from a quarry on the left, now abandoned. The softer rock was used as road infill, whereas the harder stone was used in building.

The quarry track swings sharply right and then left, descending between grassy banks and heading due north again. The path becomes ill-defined in places but eventually the fences on either side funnel the path to a gate. Pass through the gate, ford a small stream, and follow the tree-lined track to the yard with the cottage of Clwydwaunhir on the left.

Opposite the house are a small ford and a stile. Cross these and cut across some fields (SE) back to the start of the walk.

The hill vegetation comprises dwarf shrub heath and grass heath in which ling (*Calluna*) and bilberry (*Vaccinium myrtillus*) are common. Purple moor grass (*Molinia caerulea*) is abundant on flatter areas.

WALK 2
Cwm Llwch Ridge

Start	Llwynbedw, Cwm Llwch (SN006 245)
Map required	Central Map OL11
Distance	10km (6 miles)
Total ascent	620m (2035ft)

A high-level circuit of Cwm Llwch involving ascents of the two highest mountains in South Wales, Corn Du and Pen y Fan. The walk follows a horseshoe, climbing the westerly ridge to the high summits and descends the eastern ridge. The ascent is gentle at first, but the final climb to the summit of Corn Du and the descent from Pen y Fan are steep. In good weather route finding presents no problems but will certainly require the use of a map and compass in poor weather. The walk requires reasonable exertion. The main features of interest are the geomorphology, the birdlife and the superb views from the summits.

Start from the car park in a field at the end of the track from Pont Rhydybetws. There is a sign saying 'NO MOTORS'. Continue along the main track into the valley of Cwm Llwch. After about 200m there is a wood on the left. Take the path to the right and follow up the hill into the field. The path goes past deciduous woodland with alder trees on the left and comes to a stile near a large oak tree. Continue in a north-westerly direction, reaching a second wooden stile with a yellow waymark arrow and then head towards a renovated farmhouse, turning right to bypass it on your left. Looking back, and to the south, you can see into Cwm Llwch valley. On the right is the bulk of **Pen Milan** over which this route climbs.

Skirting round the farm buildings cross a stile and the field ahead to a house in the trees (Clwydwaunhir). Cross a stile and walk down the left of the hawthorn hedge to a stile and stream. After crossing the stream, turn sharp left and follow the sign to Pen Milan.

Continue between holly trees, fording the stream again and follow the track ahead to the gate with a yellow waymark arrow and the National Trust sign to Pen Milan. This

Llyn Cwm Llwch and Corn Du looking west from the summit of Pen y Fan

is where you cross the hill fence. Head due south along an indistinct path, aiming for the left side of the spur of land ahead and follow the land grooves up to the crest. A slightly sunken grassy track leads diagonally up the valley side to a path through gorse and bracken.

From here look up the valley to Pen y Fan on the left and Corn Du on the right. Far over to the east is Cefn Cwm Llwch ridge which will be your descent route. The route drops down this ridge to Twyn y Dyfnant on its left (N) edge.

Pass a group of hawthorn trees on the left and follow the old quarry track to a point where it swings sharply back to the right at the first zigzag. Continue south between small quarry spoils and keep on the main track to a flattened area of quarry debris. From here follow a walkers' path to the cairn. From the cairn there are good views to the west to Craig Cerrig-glaisiad and Fan Nedd beyond.

Walk through peat haggs to a broader section of the ridge and so to **Tommy Jones' Obelisk**. If the weather has deteriorated, a quick descent can be made from the obelisk down an obvious path to Llyn Cwm Llwch below. Otherwise,

31

Ascending Corn Du from Bwlch Duwynt

follow the ridge of Craig Cwm Llwch (SE) up the steep slope to the summit of **Corn Du**.

The final 10m or so to the summit of Corn Du involves scrambling up the Plateau Beds but a stepped path leading diagonally right will avoid further damage to these loose crags. From the top of the stepped path cross left (E) to the summit of the crags overlooking Cwm Llwch.

From the cairn follow the crags (E) and descend into the col. The path swings around (ENE) and climbs along a broad track, well marked by cairns, to the trig point on the summit of **Pen y Fan**. For a description of the mountain and its panorama see 'Geology and geomorphology of Pen y Fan,' Walk 5 and 'Pen y Fan vista,' Walk 1. The summit of Pen y Fan is the site of a Bronze Age turf barrow that contained a rectangular stone cist within which was a cremated body and a copper-alloy object.

Scramble carefully down the crags due north of the summit cairn and follow the ridge of **Cefn Cwm Llwch** for about 2km. Take a small path which leaves the main track and bears left (N) towards the pile of stones at the disused quarry of Cwar Mawr (SN018 236). From here descend west-north-west (292°) to the spur of Twyn y Dyfnant and down the steep slope to the hill fence, keeping to the right of the coniferous forestry.

Cross the fence through a gate (SN009 241) and follow the line of trees diagonally down the slope to the right. At the end of the tree line turn sharp left and drop down to the field below. An indistinct path leads directly down the field after 80m. Head for the junction of hedges to the left and continue down the slope to the ford across the stream (SN007 244) and back to the start of the walk.

CORN DU

Corn Du is the site of a Bronze Age cairn, and the stones near the edge are the remains of an excavated funerary mound (also see 'Cairn Pica,' Walk 17). Corn Du is a fine vantage point with views to the west of the Fans and, in particular, of the finely sculpted headwall of Fan Fawr to the south-west. In the valley just below to the west is Blaen Taff Fawr, the headwaters of the River Taff. The south-east presents a quite different aspect down into the valley of Neuadd with its reservoirs and continuing view towards the South Wales coast in the distance.

WALK 3
Cwm Llwch Valley

Start	Llwynbedw, Cwm Llwch (SN006 246)
Map required	Central Map OL11
Distance	6km (3.75 miles)
Total ascent	340m (1115ft)

Cwm Llwch is a beautiful valley leading from the wooded plain south of Brecon and up into the U-shaped glacial upper reaches, climbing under the spectacular head wall of Corn Du. This walk is one for a more gentle frame of mind or perhaps when conditions suggest caution in venturing too high on the mountains. No great height is reached but the atmosphere of the Beacons is savoured and the scenery is typical of the northern valleys. An early start is rewarded by the eastern sun lighting not only the valley floor and waterfalls, but also the north-eastern face of Corn Du. The walk is safe in terms of route finding and requires average fitness. Features of interest include the geology and glaciology, the plant and birdlife, waterfalls, mountain scenery and local mythology.

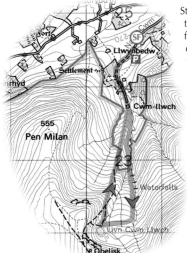

Start at the end of the car park where there is a 'NO MOTORS' sign. The ford and the hillside on the left of the car park is your descent. Follow the track leading into the valley, coming soon to another ford across the same stream, **Nant Cwm Llwch**, with a wooden bridge on the left, through a second gate and then between wooded banks with fields on either side. From here there are good views into **Cwm Llwch**, with waterfalls in the foreground and a backdrop dominated by Corn Du straight ahead and Pen y Fan on the left.

GEOLOGY AND GEOMORPHOLOGY OF CWM LLWCH

Cwm Llwch was carved by glaciers during the last ice ages but its shape is different from many of the other glacial valleys in the Beacons. The upper section is relatively flat and contains a corrie lake, Llyn Cwm Llwch, but the gradient steepens in the middle section where the waterfalls are found, before the gradient eases again near Cwm-llwch Cottage. The reason for this may be a more resistant band of rock which is also responsible for the formation of the waterfalls. The classical U shape of glacial valleys has been further modified in the middle section by two streams which have cut down into the valley floor, leaving a ridge which the main footpath follows.

The track continues southwards between old stone walls and then detours around **Cwm-llwch Cottage**. Leave the cottage on your left and skirt around the right of the farmyard by crossing over two stiles. The wide open track ahead takes a direct line up a spur of land with stream courses on either side. However, this line is of little interest and avoids the superb waterfalls glimpsed earlier. Descend instead to the left and walk along the fence which soon reaches the stream. Here a small track crosses to the left bank although either can be followed to the waterfalls.

The hill fence crosses the stream ahead but there is a low-level stride over it just before the stream divides. The left branch of the stream is the more interesting and just ahead is an impressive **waterfall**. This can be climbed on the right arriving first at a small pool above the lower fall.

Climb up the right side of the upper fall or more easily up the hill on the right of the lower fall, reaching a series of smaller waterfalls from where there are magnificent views of Corn Du. When the stream starts to break up into many smaller tributaries, leave the stream to the right, striking westwards to the corrie lake of **Llyn Cwm Llwch.**

Llyn Cwm Llwch had an **enchanted island** only accessible through a tunnel from the shore. The island rose out of the water only on May Day when fairy flowers could be gathered to fairy music. The flowers were so lovely that a sacrilegious visitor brought some away with him and down the mountain. When they faded, the island disappeared below the waters and has never been seen again.

35

From the northern end of the lake the path heads down the valley on the return walk. Descend to a cairn where the track is joined by the one from Corn Du which zigzags down from above the lake. Continue down on the crest of a spur which divides the valley into two in its upper reaches, gaining a good view of the northern end of Cwm Llwch and the agricultural areas to the north.

On reaching the hill fence, cross it by a stile alongside which is a National Trust sign for the Brecon Beacons. This is where the ascent route left the main path and crossed to the stream earlier in the walk and it is now easy to retrace your steps back to the start.

GLACIAL ORIGINS OF LLYN CWM LLWCH

Llyn Cwm Llwch is a small oligotrophic corrie lake having a surprisingly shallow maximum depth of only 8m. At a first glance, Llyn Cwm Llwch appears to have been formed by glacial ice sculpting out a deep basin in solid rock but a closer inspection reveals this is not the case. The shallowness of the lake and the hummocky mounds which surround it are the clues to its origins. The lake is situated at the head of Cwm Llwch in a spot which receives the most shade from the sun. Here, one of the last remaining blocks of ice from the Ice Age lingered on. Rock fragments were plucked from the Brownstone crags above by freeze-thaw, a process where water in fissures in the rock freezes, expands, cracking the rock and then melts, penetrating the rock even further before refreezing. These fragments tumbled over the wasting ice mass to accumulate in a ring around its edges. When the ice finally melted, a small lake dammed by the ring of moraine was left. This process is the same as in the formation of 'kettle-holes,' of which a fine example can be found beneath Craig Cerrig-gleisiad.

WALK 4
Cwm Sere and Cefn Cwm Llwch

Start	Pont y Caniedydd (SN039 244)
Map required	Central Map OL11
Distance	9.5km (6 miles)
Total ascent	560m (1841ft)

This is a fulfilling mountain route that explores one of the most spectacular and wildest valleys in the Beacons and includes sections which can be demanding in snow and ice conditions. The lower reaches of the valley are well wooded and lead into an amphitheatre created by the steep northern slopes of Cribyn and Pen y Fan. A mountain stream with small waterfalls forms a foreground to Cribyn and Pen y Fan – the two highest peaks in the Beacons. The upper parts of the route can be quite serious in bad or winter conditions but a number of less demanding variations are possible. The main features of interest are the geomorphology and glaciology, the panoramic views and some archaeological sites.

From the car parking area at Pont y Caniedydd, cross the bridge and head south up the tarmac road, passing a farm (**Bailea**) on the way. On the right of the road in Cwm Sere is a woodland nature reserve managed by the Brecknock Wildlife Trust (see 'Cwm Sere woodland,' Walk 7). At the head of this valley is the north-east face of Pen y Fan and to its left is Bryn Teg ridge.

Continue on past the turning on the left to Bailea Farm and follow the road up the hill to where it swings sharp left and through a gate. Ignore this turning and follow the stony track for 250m straight ahead to a gate in the hill fence on the far side of which is a National Trust sign for Cwm Cynwyn. The ridge on the right is the descent route leading towards the end of the walk.

The stony track you have just walked along is part of the Roman Road that leads to Bwlch ar y Fan (see Walk 11). The Scots pines (*Pinus Sylvestris*) immediately on the left as you cross the hill fence may have been planted as route indicators to drovers and, if this is the case, would

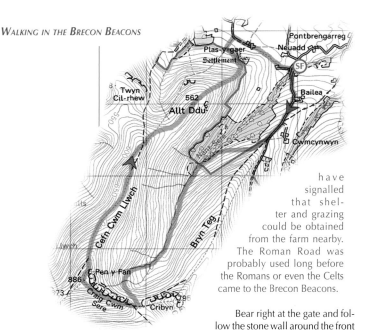

have signalled that shelter and grazing could be obtained from the farm nearby. The Roman Road was probably used long before the Romans or even the Celts came to the Brecon Beacons.

Bear right at the gate and follow the stone wall around the front of Bryn Teg and into the valley of **Cwm Sere**. After about 400m the stone wall has collapsed (SN033 234) Just after this point drop gradually across the slope until the stream course is reached. Follow

Nant Sere

the stream course, either by scrambling along the bank or by staying on more even ground above, following a convenient sheep track.

Once in the basin below Cribyn, strike across towards the foot of the north-east face of **Pen y Fan** and from here climb the headwall by the track which starts from bottom right and continues to top left. You will cross piles of stones brought down the gullies by the winter frosts. The headwall track rises at an easy angle, presenting no problems, and arrives at the unnamed **col** between Cribyn and Pen y Fan. There is a good view of Cribyn during the ascent.

From the col, climb steadily (W) following the line of **Craig Cwm Sere** to the summit of Pen y Fan. In early spring the vibrant colours of rare arctic-alpines may be seen on the most inaccessible crags.

FLORA OF NORTH-EAST FACE OF PEN Y FAN

This steep, impregnable face protects one of Britain's true botanical treasures from grazing sheep. The combination of high altitude and a shaded northern aspect creates living conditions more akin to polar latitudes than to temperate southern Britain. Extensive ledges high up on the face are crammed full of interesting and unusual species which bring the otherwise bleak and foreboding crags alive with vibrant colour in spring. Interesting plants include roseroot (*Sedum rosea*), rock stonecrop (*Sedum forsteranum*), mossy saxifrage (*Saxifraga hypnoides*), purple saxifrage (*Saxifraga oppositifolia*), vernal sandwort (*Minuartia verna*), sea campion (*Silena maritima*), Wilson's filmy fern (*Hymenophyllum wilsonii*), globe flower (*Trollius europaeus*), serrated wintergreen, green spleenwort (*Asplenium viride*), lesser meadow rue (*Thalictrum minus*), brittle bladder-fern (*Cystopteris fragilis*) and northern bedstraw (*Galium boreale*). These ledges also support an unusual collection of bryophytes and several upland invertebrate species, including a rare arctic aphid. These plants and animals are highly specialised to be able to survive in these extreme conditions.

Looking back down Cwm Sere from the approach to Pen y Fan, there is an ideal view of its geomorphology. Cwm Sere was carved by ice into a U-shape but this has been altered slightly since the last Ice Age. On the left there is a distinct step in the valley side, a post-glacial feature known as an 'antiplanation terrace', while **Nant Sere** has been eroding away a notch in its base (see 'Glacial origins of U-shaped valleys,' Introduction).

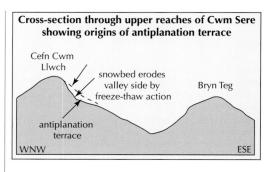

Cross-section through upper reaches of Cwm Sere showing origins of antiplanation terrace

Cefn Cwm Llwch

snowbed erodes valley side by freeze-thaw action

Bryn Teg

antiplanation terrace

WNW

ESE

An **antiplanation terrace** is formed when a snowbed develops on a sheltered step in a valley side. This snowbed erodes into the hillside by freeze-thaw action (see 'Glacial origins of Llyn Cwm Llwch,' Walk 3), depositing material further downslope. In the case of the western side of Cwm Sere, a minor platform was formed due to differences in resistance to erosion of underlying rock types and, in fact, this antiplanation terrace may be related to the change from Brownstones to the underlying Senni Beds (see 'Geology of the Brecon Beacons,' Introduction).

Looking up the slope the flat-capped summit of Corn Du can be seen, and to the left is Bwlch Duwynt, which means 'Windy Gap'. The final ascent to the summit of Pen y Fan is up a very stony area and The National Trust has built a zigzag path up this face to the top. The crags here are made of Plateau Beds that form a distinctive cap to the summits of Pen y Fan and Corn Du (see 'Geology of the Brecon Beacons,' Introduction).

Walk across the flat surface of Pen y Fan, which is also badly eroded, to the trig point. This can be found in bad visibility by carefully following the north-east crag line. The trig point is at the end of this to the left. The north-east face is very steep and care must be taken not to stray too near the edge, especially in strong south-westerly winds or when corniced in winter. The summit is the site of an Iron Age cairn and there are good views and photographic opportunities from here. For details of the geomorphology of Pen y Fan, see 'Geology and geomorphology of Pen y Fan,' Walk 5.

The slope of the summit surface is the key to the dip of the resistant Plateau Beds which cap the summit (see 'Geology of the Brecon Beacons,' Introduction). The summit is, in fact, the **dip slope** of this rock formation which lies unconformably on the Brownstones, but the general trend in dip of all the rock strata in this area is to the south. A slight component of the dip controls the drainage in the valley sides, favouring the eastern facing slopes. A close look at the map reveals this to be true for the majority of the gullies in Cwm Sere and Cwm Cynwyn.

Leave the summit of Pen y Fan by carefully scrambling (NNE) down the exposed Plateau Beds. The rocks can be slippery but the route drops quickly to the fine ridge of **Cefn Cwm Llwch**. ▶

Below to the left is the valley of Cwm Llwch and the lake of Llyn Cwm Llwch (see 'Glacial origins of Llyn Cwm Llwch,' Walk 3). Looking down to the right you will see a large gully which holds a frothy white cataract after heavy rain.

Cribyn and Pen y Fan from above Cwm Llwch

As you scramble down from the summit, look carefully at the upper surfaces of the near horizontal Plateau Beds for ripple marks (see Walk 1).

41

Cwm Sere from the summit of Pen y Fan, showing the antiplanation terrace on the eastern flank of Cefn Cwm Llwch

Once on the flat section of the ridge, look across to the east for a magnificent view over the ridges of the Beacons and the triangular profile of Cribyn. Looking through the gap between Cribyn and Pen y Fan, you can see the bluff of the ridge which leads down on the right-hand side of the Neuadd Valley. Turning to the entrance of Cwm Sere, there is a pleasant woodland area which is managed by the Brecknock Wildlife Trust (see Walk 7).

Follow the path along the flat ridge, leaving it when it drops gradually to the valley of Cwm Gwdi. Keep to the eastern edge of the ridge, following a path through some boggy areas with mainly heather, past the disused quarries and onwards to **Allt Ddu**.

From the spur of Cefn Cwm Llwch, which is very well populated with skylarks in spring and summer, there is a good view looking back to Pen y Fan with Cribyn on the left and Corn Du sticking through the gap in the ridge. As you descend this route further you can see the town of Brecon over to the left beyond the end of the ridge. There is an area of heather and bilberry with the odd pool in the peat. At the end of this ridge is a number of hummocks and hollows, part of an old quarry, and you can look down past a rowan tree growing out of the crags to Cwmcynwyn Farm. There is a rock outcrop here with bedding showing clearly.

From the pools on the summit of Allt Ddu drop down past the stones of the quarry towards the **Plas-y-gaer settlement**. Just on the edge of this hill there is a distinctive furrow in the hillside which is an old quarry path. Continue down this path (marked with a dotted line on the map) towards the settlement, descending the front of the ridge. The descent of this ridge provides a good view of the settlement with the earth bank being now planted with a line of large trees.

Plas-y-gaer is an **Iron Age settlement** some 2000 years old, *gaer* meaning fortress and *plas* meaning place. The site is unexcavated but was probably built to defend the surrounding fertile land. There are surviving earthworks forming an oval shape and the height of the main rampart varies between 2 and 3.2m. As there is no sign of an entrance, access was probably gained from the north. No ancient features are visible in the interior.

At the bottom of the slope turn left in front of the settlement. As you come round the corner of the settlement follow the path diagonally down to the left, arriving at a stone wall, where there is a finger post and gate. A track leads to the farm (Plas-y-gaer). At the farm turn left through a gate and right into a field at the blue waymark post.

From here head across the field to a line of pylons reached through a gap in the trees. Turn right at a line of trees and walk up to a gate and stile in the right corner of the field. After crossing the stile, descend a shallow valley to another stile which you will see in the field about 60m in front of you. Follow the wire fence on the right-hand side downslope to the derelict buildings. Walk to the left of the farm buildings to a stile in a fence and onto a track. At the end of the farm track is a gate beyond which is a tarmac road. Turn right on the road and drop down the hill to the start at Pont Caniedydd.

WALK 5

Cwm Sere and Bryn Teg

Start	Pont y Caniedydd (SN039 244)
Map required	Central Map OL11
Distance	11km (6.5 miles)
Total ascent	641m (2103ft)

A classic route from the north side of the Beacons and well worth choosing for a first visit. It includes a superb valley walk with small waterfalls, a climb up the head wall, a detour to the highest peak of Pen y Fan, return via Cribyn and the Bryn Teg ridge. There are good views of the Beacons themselves, the Black Mountains and even of Cadair Idris to the north on a clear day. Route finding, as in all high places, may require map and compass and the final climb to the summits can be hard going. There is particular interest in the glacial geomorphology of the U-shaped valleys.

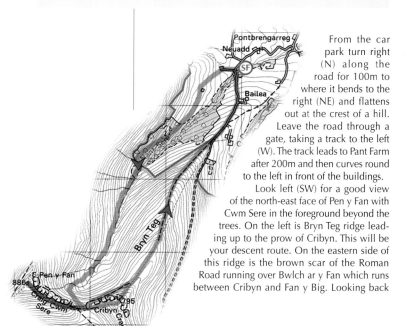

From the car park turn right (N) along the road for 100m to where it bends to the right (NE) and flattens out at the crest of a hill. Leave the road through a gate, taking a track to the left (W). The track leads to Pant Farm after 200m and then curves round to the left in front of the buildings.

Look left (SW) for a good view of the north-east face of Pen y Fan with Cwm Sere in the foreground beyond the trees. On the left is Bryn Teg ridge leading up to the prow of Cribyn. This will be your descent route. On the eastern side of this ridge is the brown scar of the Roman Road running over Bwlch ar y Fan which runs between Cribyn and Fan y Big. Looking back the way you have walked, the escarpments of the Black Mountains are visible on a clear day.

Continue on this track, leaving the buildings on your right, and climb steadily up the slope through a gap between hawthorn hedges. Bear right and then left, continuing in the direction of Cwm Sere to Croftau. Leave the house on your left, pass through the gate and a large oak on the right and keep to the left-hand side of the field to another gate where you enter **Cwm Sere** proper. The woodland on the far side of the stream on your left is managed by the Brecknock Wildlife Trust (see Walk 7).

Continue through yet another gate along the obvious track leading into sparse woodland and across to a gap in the tree line. Continue across the field for 300m to a line of trees in front of you. In the centre of this barrier is a gate leading to a track which bears slightly right past moss-covered ant hills and through mixed woodland of beech and hazel. ▶

The track is easily followed as it drops through the woods, crossing a small stream running down from the right. At the end of the woodland is the hill fence through which a gate leads out onto the hillside, opening up a magnificent view of Cribyn on the left and Pen y Fan straight in front.

Deciduous woodland attracts varied birdlife and, depending upon the time of day and season, you may see woodpeckers and owls as well as other typical woodland species.

Pen y Fan from Cribyn

Drop into the stream bed and follow this upstream, encountering small waterfalls on the way towards the headwall at the end of Cwm Sere between the north faces of Pen y Fan on the right and Cribyn on the left.

You can expect to see dippers in the stream bed and, with luck, a buzzard wheeling overhead or a heron hunting its prey near the water. Cwm Sere was carved by ice into a U-shape but this has been altered slightly by a snowbed eating away at its western side in post-glacial times (see Walk 4) and by Nant Sere eroding away a notch in its base (see 'Glacial origin of U-shaped valleys,' Introduction).

Once in the basin below Cribyn strike across towards the foot of the north-east face of **Pen y Fan**. The sheer immensity of the north-east face of Pen y Fan can be fully appreciated from the head of the cwm.

GEOLOGY AND GEOMORPHLOGY OF PEN Y FAN

The north-east face of Pen y Fan rises some 380m (1200ft), becoming vertical near the top where the more resistant Plateau Beds form a distinctive cap to the summit. Units of the Lower Old Red Sandstone, Plateau Beds and Brownstones are well exposed in the face. The ribbed nature of the Brownstones is due to the alternation of sandstone with softer marls. The brown scars on the face of the mountain are testimony to the relentless onslaught of the elements and the processes of erosion. The most deadly of these is freezing and thawing of water in cracks in the rocks, which literally shatters the stone along existing lines of weakness. (The Brownstones are particularly well bedded and cleaved, and split apart forming regular blocks, seemingly made for constructing dry-stone walls and buildings.) Gravity then plays its part in transporting stone and soil downslope. Rainwater percolates into the ground where it is concentrated along the upper surfaces of the less permeable marly layers. Eventually it seeps out of the face, leading to erosion of the soft marls. This undermines the sandstone blocks above, leading to their collapse. This water is then concentrated in gullies, further eroding soil and rock which is then channelled to the bottom of the face, where it spreads out to form talus cones. Look out for a distinctive white, frothy stream which forms in the large gully on the right of the face after heavy rain. In snow and ice conditions, the gullies provide distinctive winter climbing routes for daring climbers using crampons and ice axes.

Ascending the steep prow of Cribyn

From the foot of Pen y Fan take the track up the head-wall which goes from bottom right to top left. Crossing piles of loose stones at first, the headwall track rises at an easy angle, presenting no problems, and arrives at the unnamed col between Cribyn and Pen y Fan. ▶

The extended route to the summit of Pen y Fan leaves from here. There is also an exhilarating alternative route round the shoulder of Cribyn that may be followed from here.

Turn left (E) up the steep, eroded slope to the summit of **Cribyn**. The ascent of Cribyn is rewarded with an impressive panorama on a clear day, with good views to the west of the north-east face of Pen y Fan and to the east of the other Beacons valleys and ridges, Fan y Big and the Black Mountains beyond.

Descend (NNE) following the narrow prow of Cribyn. The steep descent down the nose of Cribyn can be exciting in snow and ice conditions and may well require crampons and an ice axe. Stop now and again to enjoy the views – look over into the adjacent valley of Cwm Cynwyn through which runs the Roman Road (see Walk 11) up to Bwlch ar y Fan between Cribyn and Fan y Big.

The return route heads down **Bryn Teg** (NNE) on a wide grassy track to a gate past a sign reading 'Entry to National Trust Land' (Bannau Brycheiniog – The Brecon Beacons). Follow the stony track, part of the Roman Road, which leads down to a crossroads where you take the road ahead. This leads back to the stone bridge from where you started.

Extension
Climb W along Craig Cwm Sere to the summit of Pen y Fan. The final ascent of Pen y Fan is badly eroded but the National Trust has built a zigzag path out of the Brownstones to reduce further damage. Now descend back to the unnamed col between Pen y Fan and Cribyn and rejoin Walk 5.

Alternative route
Traverse around the shoulder of Cribyn along a sheep track. This is the most exciting mountain route in the Beacons, the narrowness of the path and the steep drops giving the walker a real taste of exposure. Remember that great care must be exercised here in winter conditions where crampons and an ice axe may well be the order of the day. Look back now and again at the north-east face of Pen y Fan which dominates the skyline, making this one of the finest viewpoints in the Beacons. The final part of this traverse affords grand views of Cwm Sere and across Allt Ddu to the town of Brecon on the left. (See Walk 6 for a description of the flora of the north-west face of Cribyn). Now rejoin Walk 5 at the start of Bryn Teg.

WALK 6
Cwm Sere Ridge

Start	Pont y Caniedydd (SN039 244)
Map required	Central Map OL11
Distance	10km (6 miles)
Total ascent	560m (1841ft)

This is one of the classic ridge walks in the Beacons. The route climbs the ridge on the east side of the valley and includes ascents of Cribyn and the highest peak in the Beacons, Pen y Fan. Descent is via Cefn Cwm Llwch, the ridge on the western border of the valley. The ascents and descents in the upper reaches are steep and good walking fitness is essential. Interesting features include a nature reserve, the mountain geology and excellent views of all the high peaks and the valleys associated with them.

From the car parking area at Pont y Caniedydd turn south-east, cross over the bridge and up the lane ahead. On the right of the road into the valley of **Cwm Sere** is a woodland nature reserve managed by the Brecknock Wildlife Trust (see Walk 7).

> Nant Sere drains the vast cauldron formed by the head-walls of Cribyn and Pen y Fan. Water avens and mossy saxifrage grow on the banks of this mountain stream which then flows on through ash, alder and birch wood-land. Cwm Sere is extremely rich in flora and fauna with over 200 species of flowering plants and ferns, abundant fungi, birds and insects, at least two of which are rare arctic-alpine species.

Continue past the turning on the left to **Bailea Farm**, and follow the road up the hill to where it swings sharp left and through a gate. Ignore this turning and follow the stony track, the old Roman Road (see Walk 11), for 250m straight ahead to a gate in the hill fence, on the far side of which is a National Trust sign for Cwm Cynwyn.

On the left is the ridge of Cefn Cyff which leads down from Fan y Big and straight ahead is the ridge of **Bryn Teg** which you are about to ascend to the summit of Cribyn. On the right is Cefn Cwm Llwch which leads down from Pen y Fan and this will be your descent route.

Continuing from this point at the hill fence, ignore the stony track which goes off to the left and head straight for the ridge ahead of you. After a concentrated pull up the beginning of this ridge you arrive at a cairn. The ridge ascends in three main steps and after

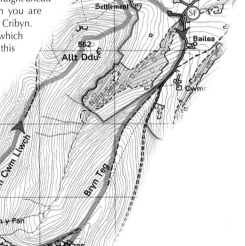

49

Pen y Fan from Bryn Teg

The alternative route to Pen y Fan leaves from here.

the second major climb you arrive at a level section marked by a second cairn. The final step is the ascent of the prow of **Cribyn**. ◀

> The step in the middle of the ridge has formed due to the underlying geology. This step is known as a secondary scarp and results from a change from Brownstones to Senni Beds.

Climb the narrow path to the summit of Cribyn, then descend west along a distinct eroded path to the col. To the south is the Neuadd Valley where two small reservoirs dam the Blaen Taf Fechan, which is fed by surface run-off and ground-water collected in this basin.

From the col, climb steadily (W) following the line of **Craig Cwm Sere** to the summit of Pen y Fan. The final ascent to the summit of Pen y Fan is up a very stony area and The National Trust has built a zigzag path up this face to the top.

Walk across the flat surface of Pen y Fan, which is also badly eroded, to the trig point. This can be found in bad visibility by carefully following the north-east crag line. The trig point is at the end of this to the left. The north-east face is very steep and care must be taken not to stray too near the edge, especially in strong south-westerly winds or when corniced in winter.

Leave the summit of Pen y Fan by carefully scrambling (NNE) down the exposed Plateau Beds. The rocks can be slippery but the route drops quickly to the fine ridge of **Cefn Cwm Llwch**.

Follow the path along the flat section of the ridge, leaving it when it drops gradually to the valley of Cwm Gwdi. Keep to the eastern edge of the ridge, following a path through some boggy areas with mainly heather, past the disused quarries and onwards to **Allt Ddu**.

From the pools on the summit of Allt Ddu drop down past the stones of the quarry towards the **Plas-y-gaer settlement**. Just on the edge of this hill there is a distinctive furrow in the hillside which is an old quarry path. Continue down this path (marked with a dotted line on the map) towards the settlement, descending the front of the ridge. The descent of this ridge provides a good view of the settlement with the earth bank being now planted with a line of large trees.

Blaen Taf Fechan and the Upper Neuadd Reservoir

51

At the bottom of the slope turn left in front of the settlement. As you come round the corner of the settlement follow the path diagonally down to the left, arriving at a stone wall. There is a finger post and gate. A track leads to the farm (Plas-y-gaer). At the farm turn left through a gate and right into a field at the blue waymark post.

From here head across the field to a line of pylons reached through a gap in the trees. Turn right at a line of trees and walk up to a gate and stile in the right corner of the field. After crossing the stile, descend a shallow valley to another stile which you will see in the field about 60m in front of you. Follow the wire fence on the right-hand side downslope to the derelict buildings. Walk to the left of the farm buildings to a stile in a fence and onto a track. At the end of the farm track is a gate beyond which is a tarmac road. Turn right on the road and down the hill to the start at Pont y Caniedydd.

Alternative route

Follow the Cribyn face path off to your right leading to the col between Cribyn and Pen y Fan.

> The further you travel, the steeper the cliff becomes with the Brownstones becoming more prominent up to your left. These are responsible for forming the red soil of the path. On a still day you will often hear the sound of croaking ravens high above you.

Towards the end of the path, as you cross a number of small gullies, there are quite steep drops away to the right and the path surface becomes uneven and stepped. As you are walking along this path the views of the main face of Pen y Fan change and become even more impressive (see 'Geology and geomorphology of Pen y Fan,' Walk 5). This path can be dangerous in winter conditions and crampons and ice axe may be needed.

FLORA OF NORTH-WEST FACE OF CRIBYN

Ledges of this face are more accessible to sheep grazing than those of the north-east face of Pen y Fan and so the interesting arctic-alpine plants are not so prolific. Nevertheless, roseroot (*Sedum rosea*), mossy saxifrage (*Saxifraga hypnoides*), purple saxifrage (*Saxifraga oppositifolia*), and vernal sandwort (*Minuartia verna*) are common. Rock stonecrop (*Sedum forsteranum*) can be found but is more localised. Other species include cowberry (*Vaccinium vitis-idaea*), green spleenwort (*Asplenium viride*), brittle bladder-fern (*Cystopteris fragilis*), limestone bedstraw (*Galium sterneri*), viviparous fescue (*Festuca vivipara*), great wood-rush (*Luzula sylvatica*), cowslip (*Primula veris*), common wild thyme (*Thymus drucei*) and northern bedstraw (*Galium boreale*). The wet ledges also support an excellent collection of upland bryophytes.

WALK 7
Cwm Sere Valley

Start	Pont y Caniedydd (SN039 244)
Map required	Central Map OL11
Distance	6.25km (3.6 miles)
Total ascent	250m (820ft)

A low-level walk around one of the most beautiful and spectacular of the Welsh valleys. The sheer size and steepness of the impressive north-east face of Pen y Fan can be fully appreciated from the head of Cwm Sere. Like all valley walks there is little danger of getting lost, even in poor weather, and it can be enjoyed with a leisurely approach requiring not too much exertion. The main features of interest are the geological features of the headwalls and north-eastern faces, the glacial valleys and the woodlands.

From the car park turn right (N) along the road for 100m to where it bends to the right (NE) and flattens out at the crest of a hill. Leave the road through a gate, taking a track to the left (W). The track leads to Pant Farm after 200m and then curves round to the left in front of the buildings.

Continue on this track, leaving the buildings on your right, and climb steadily up the slope through a gap between hawthorn hedges. Bear right and then left, continuing in the

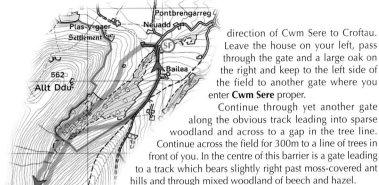

direction of Cwm Sere to Croftau. Leave the house on your left, pass through the gate and a large oak on the right and keep to the left side of the field to another gate where you enter **Cwm Sere** proper.

Continue through yet another gate along the obvious track leading into sparse woodland and across to a gap in the tree line. Continue across the field for 300m to a line of trees in front of you. In the centre of this barrier is a gate leading to a track which bears slightly right past moss-covered ant hills and through mixed woodland of beech and hazel.

The track is easily followed as it drops through the woods, crossing a small stream running down from the right. At the end of the woodland is the hill fence through which a gate leads out onto the hillside, opening up a magnificent view of Cribyn on the left and Pen y Fan straight in front. Drop into the stream bed and follow this upstream, encountering small waterfalls on the way towards the headwall at the end of Cwm Sere between the north faces of Pen y Fan on the right and Cribyn on the left.

Cwm Sere and Pen y Fan

Cross over the stream and make your way back down the eastern side of the valley. The going is easier if you keep above the steep-sided stream gully, making use of the occasional sheep track. Eventually, the hill fence forces you above the stream and guides you to the gate where you meet the Roman Road. Take the stony track for 250m where you bear left when you meet a road.

CWM SERE WOODLAND

The woods on the eastern bank of Nant Sere are leased from the National Trust by the Brecknock Wildlife Trust and 42 acres are managed as a nature reserve. Even though it has been heavily grazed in the past, the majority of the trees appear to be very old. Parts of the woodland are very wet and these areas are dominated by alder. A particularly rich collection of insects, liverworts and fungi thrives in these boggy conditions where rotting wood is abundant. Drier areas of woodland are populated with ash, rowan, cherry, field maple and sessile oak. Brown birch is common near the top of the wood. Woodland birds are numerous and include willow warblers and redstarts with a surprisingly large rookery located in a clump of birches. Open glades in the wood are ideal habitats for species such as pied flycatchers. The reserve has a wide range of invertebrates including a number of specialities such as a rare lace-wing fly and rare craneflies. All in all, this reserve is a fascinating area, the combinations of damp and dry woodland and damp and dry glades resulting in a great variety of plant and animal species.

Follow this road down the hill and so back to the start just across Pont y Caniedydd.

WALK 8
Cwm Cynwyn and Bryn Teg

Start	Pont y Caniedydd (SN039 244)
Map required	Central Map OL11
Distance	8km (5 miles)
Total ascent	641m (2102ft)

The route enters Cwm Cynwyn and crosses the stream to the other side of the valley, avoiding the busy and rather monotonous walk along the Roman Road. An ascent of Cribyn via Craig Cwm Cynwyn is followed by an exciting descent along the prow of Cribyn and an easy walk back along Bryn Teg ridge. The headwall ascent to Cribyn and the first part of the descent to Bryn Teg are steep. Adverse weather makes the use of map and compass mandatory, and in snow and ice conditions crampons are desirable. The walk is quite energetic. A nature reserve, the glacial nature of the valley, the views from Cribyn and the Roman Road are the main points of interest.

Cross the bridge and head south up the road, passing **Bailea Farm** on the way. On the right of the road in the valley of Cwm Sere is a woodland nature reserve (see Walk 7) and at the head of this valley is the north-east face of Pen y Fan. To its left is Bryn Teg ridge. Ignore the turning on the left to Bailea Farm and follow the road up the hill to where it swings sharp left and through a gate. Ignore this turning and follow the stony track straight ahead to a gate in the hill fence on the far side of which is a National Trust sign for Cwm Cynwyn. This stony track is popularly known as the **Roman Road** (see Walk 11).

Fifty metres on the left is a gate which leads into a walled enclosure at the end of which is a second gate. Follow through these and down the rough track to another gate and so to the farm (New Cwmcynwyn) via the lane to the right. Pass through the farmyard to a gate and through this to a stony lane where ahead is a fine view of Fan y Big. At the bottom of this stony lane the track bears to the right up the valley. Ignore this and continue dropping down left alongside the green moss-covered stone wall to the stream.

Cross the river, aiming for the gate opposite. In spate, this river may be very difficult to cross. If so, retrace to the stony lane south of **New Cwmcynwyn**

56

Farm and continue up the right side of the stream rejoining the route at the stone sheep pens.

Keep left up the hill to the top and round to the right into the grounds of Old Cwmcynwyn Farm.

Cwm Cynwyn and the Black Mountains from Bryn Teg

The fireplace still has its oak lintel in place and a surprisingly large tree emerges halfway up the front of the chimney breast. Its roots have penetrated through the stones and into the ground below.

From the ruins turn left by the wire fence and up the track to a stile and so to the path running along the hillside 50m above. Turn right (SSW), following the path towards the head of the valley. The hill fence turns right and drops down to the river bed.

In front of you on the right is the prow of Cribyn and the ridge running round from that to the gap of the Roman Road and Fan y Big on your left.

Continue along the east side of the valley above the stream down to the right. Eventually the indistinct path you are following meets the stream bed at a hawthorn tree and old stone enclosures (hafodydd).

The ruined stone enclosures in this area were originally small buildings and pens, called **hafodydd**, used when flocks were moved to higher pastures in the spring. One stone is inscribed with 'G.H.', the initials of the Gwynne Halfords of Buckland, a large land-owning family in Victorian times.

Leave the stream course here and strike up left onto the lower reaches of Fan y Big on which there is a double row of small rock outcrops which should be passed on the left-hand side. Traverse right above the lower outcrops and climb steadily to the Roman Road.

You will want to catch your breath after this sustained climb and there are plenty of interesting features to see from this good viewpoint. Down below in the head of the valley is an interesting glacial feature (see 'Head of Cwm Cynwyn'). Up above to the west is the impressive crag of Craig Cwm Cynwyn (see Walk 10) formed from resistant Brownstones (see 'Geology of the Brecon Beacons,' Walk 21). Finally, you may well be resting on a once busy Roman thoroughfare.

Looking along Craig Cwm Cynwyn to the summits of Cribyn and Pen y Fan

HEAD OF CWM CYNWYN

The hummocky terrain in the head of Cwm Cynwyn is an interesting glacial feature. This was deposited by melting glaciers and consists of angular and rounded boulders in a sandy, clayey matrix which is known as boulder-clay. A marshy area below the headwall crags is where the corrie lake would once have been. Hare's tail grass (*Eriophorum vaginatum*), soft rush (*Juncus effusus*) and sphagnum (*Sphagnum recurvum*) now thrive in the wet conditions.

Turn left at the Roman Road and make your way to Bwlch ar y Fan, the 'Gap between the Peaks'. This is an ideal place to appreciate the almost perfect U-shape of this glacial valley (see Introduction).

From here climb west up **Craig Cwm Cynwyn** to the summit of **Cribyn.** The lower part is the steepest pull but the slope becomes easier as you approach the summit.

From Cribyn descend steeply along the **Bryn Teg** ridge northwards down to the National Trust sign and so back down the road to the start. The steeper section in the middle of the ridge is a secondary scarp formed by the transition from Brownstones to underlying Senni Beds (see 'Geology of the Brecon Beaons,' Walk 21).

WALK 9
Cwm Cynwyn and Cefn Cyff

Start	Pen-yr-heol (SN058 241)
Map required	Central Map OL11
Distance	8.75km (5.2 miles)
Total ascent	410m (1350ft)

A fairly easy walk during which you can enjoy the beautiful valley of Cwm Cynwyn and the return via the ridge of Cefn Cyff. Deciduous woodland fills the lower reaches, giving a natural, timeless atmosphere. The valley provides easy walking but a degree of exertion is required for the final climb up to the 'Gap' (Bwlch ar y Fan) and to Fan y Big. Interest is sustained by the plants and birds of the valley, the river scenery, the geological features and the views from Fan y Big, which are among the most impressive in the Beacons.

Start at the holiday cottages (Pen-yr-heol) just past the houses of **Rhiwiau** and Llyn Fron. From the car park at the end of the road take a little time to enjoy the views east of Cwm Oergwm. Do not go into the yard in front of the buildings but turn up the obvious stony track on the right (SW) to a gate which leads to the open hillside.

Cross over the hill fence and follow the path which divides into two after a short distance. Take the main obvious track rising up the hillside to the left, avoiding the small track which appears to go down into Cwm Cynwyn on your right. The large track immediately divides again and the main track goes further up to the left. Ignore this and go straight ahead, contouring around the hill. The hill fence swings away down to the right, marked by a large birch tree on the corner.

Look back from here for a very good view of the Black Mountains stretching up to Hay-on-Wye. The track is well marked and runs through bracken on the upslope side of the old hill wall and newer hill fence. Straight ahead you first see Pen y Fan with Cefn Cwm Llwch leading up to it.

The hill fence drops away to the right. Continuing around the contour of the hill, cross a small stream and come to a group of hawthorn trees, with a good view up to Cribyn on the left and Pen y Fan to the right.

The view south-west to the head of the valley shows the ice-sculpted U-shape and the steep headwall (see 'Glacial origin of U-shaped valleys,' Introduction). The notch in the col, called Bwlch ar y Fan or the Gap between the Peaks, is where the Roman Road reaches its highest point before dropping into the Taf Fechan Valley.

Continue contouring across the slope and arrive at a stile over the hill fence on your right. You can make a detour from the path over this stile to the derelict buildings of **Old Cwmcynwyn Farm** as these are well worth a visit (see Walk 8).

From the ruins, retrace the path over the stile and turn to the right along the path above the hill fence. This path contours the hillside and into the stream bed.

Across the valley to the right is Bryn Teg ridge with its secondary scarp (see 'Geology of the Brecon Beacons,' Introduction) and the Roman Road running beneath it. This ridge leads up to the prow of Cribyn. Beyond it is Cefn Cwm Llwch ridge. Behind you to your left as you look up Cwm Cynwyn Valley is the ridge of Cefn Cyff, the return route.

The Beacons summits from Craig Cwmoergwm

Cwm Cynwyn from Bwlch ar y Fan

The walk up the valley is most enjoyable. Hawthorn trees are dotted around on the grassy slopes of the upper valley and the level sheep tracks make a criss-cross pattern with the steep gullies created by water run-off. The head of the valley is formed by the steep slope of Fan y Big to the left and the higher crags of Cribyn to the right.

Scramble along the stream towards the head of the valley. Leave the stream and strike up left onto the lower reaches of **Fan y Big** on which is a double row of small rock outcrops which should be passed on the left-hand side. Traverse right above the lower outcrops and climb steadily to the Roman Road and so on to the Gap (**Bwlch ar y Fan**).

There are many features to be seen from this good viewpoint. Down in the head of this U-shaped valley is an interesting glacial feature (see 'Head of Cwm Cynwyn,' Walk 8; Glacial origins of U-shaped Valleys, Introduction). Up above to the west is the impressive crag of Craig Cwm Cynwyn (see Walk 10) formed from resistant Brownstones (see 'Geology of the Brecon Beacons,' Introduction). Finally, you may well be resting on a once busy Roman thoroughfare.

Head east up the steep slope following the line of the crags to the summit of Fan y Big. Descend gradually (NNE) along the obvious ridge of **Cefn Cyff** which drops more steeply after 1.5km.

The step in the ridge is a result of the underlying rock formations and is a secondary scarp formed by the transition from Brownstones to underlying Senni Beds (see 'Geology of the Brecon Beacons,' Introduction).

The path becomes steeper again after another 1.2km of fairly flat ground and drops north-east to a gate in the hill fence. Pass through this and follow a stony track back to the start by the sheep dip and pens.

WALK 10
Cwm Cynwyn Ridge

Start	Pen-yr-heol (SN058 240)
Map required	Central Map OL11
Distance	8km (5 miles)
Total ascent	605m (1985ft)

A high-level clockwise circuit of the ridges around Cwm Cynwyn. The route climbs steadily along Cefn Cyff and then more steeply to the summit of Fan y Big. A short descent is followed by a sustained climb to the impressive summit of Cribyn, before one of the steepest descents in the Beacons to the ridge of Bryn Teg. All high ridges in the Beacons can be subject to rapid weather deterioration, and a compass and map and the ability to use them are important. Two high peaks are included, demanding reasonable fitness. The glacial valleys and panoramas from the summits provide interest throughout the walk.

Start at the holiday cottages (Pen-yr-heol) beyond the houses of **Rhiwiau** and Llyn Fron. Do not go into the yard in front of the buildings but turn up the obvious stony track on the right (SW) to a gate which leads to the open hillside. Head

CEFN CYFF

Towards the northern end of Cefn Cyff, the view south-west is of the valleys and ridges leading up to the summits. The steeper section in the middle of the ridge is a secondary scarp formed by the transition from Brownstones to underlying Senni Beds (see 'Geology of the Brecon Beacons,' Introduction). The top of the ridge is covered in heavily grazed blanket mire which is mostly hare's tail grass (*Eriophorum vaginatum*) with some ling (*Calluna*), deer grass (*Trichophorum cespitosum*) and bilberry (*Vaccinium myrtilius*). The sides of the ridge are covered in heath rush/mat grass (*Juncus squarrosus*/*Nardus*) grassland which grades into mat grass on lower slopes and then into bracken.

straight up the ridge ahead, Cefn Cyff, eventually picking up a distinctive path marked by two cairns. Continue along the ridge to the summit of **Fan y Big.**

Descend west to the Gap (Bwlch ar y Fan). Look below to the north for a good view of the head of Cwm Cynwyn (see Walk 8). From here climb west up **Craig Cwm Cynwyn** to the summit of **Cribyn.** The lower part is the steepest pull and the slope becomes easier as you approach the summit. From this ridge you have a superb view north of the perfect U-shaped valley of Cwm Cynwyn.

From Cribyn descend steeply along the **Bryn Teg ridge** northwards towards a gate in the hill fence and a National Trust sign. Notice the step halfway along the ridge. It has the same origins as the step you ascended earlier on Cefn Cyff (see 'Geology of the Brecon Beacons,' Introduction).

Fifty metres before this on the right is a gate which leads into a walled enclosure at the end of which is a second gate.

CRAIG CWM CYNWYN

The crags beneath Craig Cwm Cynwyn are accessible to grazing sheep and so are not as botanically interesting as the Pen y Fan and Cribyn headwalls, especially the highest ledges of the sheer north-east face of Pen y Fan. Vegetation consists mostly of mixed acidic grassland and purple moor grass (*Vaccinium*) heath on slopes and ledges between rock faces. The most inaccessible ledges are oases for herb-rich communities which include *Scabiosa columbaria*, mossy saxifrage (*Saxifraga hypnoides*), viviparous fescue (*Festuca vivipara*), brittle bladder fern (*Cystopteris fragilis*) and limestone bedstraw (*Galium sterneri*).

Follow through these and down the rough track to another gate and so to the farm (**New Cwmcynwyn**) via the lane to the right. Pass through the farmyard to a gate and through this to a stony lane where ahead is a fine view of Fan y Big. At the bottom of this stony lane the track bears to the right up the valley. Ignore this and drop down left alongside the green moss-covered stone wall to the stream.

Cross the river aiming for the gate opposite and, keeping left,

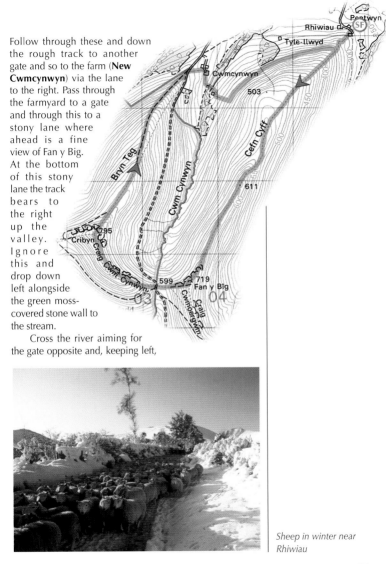

Sheep in winter near Rhiwiau

65

*Pen y Fan and Corn Du
from Cribyn*

go up the hill to the top and round to the right into the grounds of Old Cwmcynwyn Farm. From the ruins turn left by the wire fence and up the track to a stile and so to the path running along the hillside 50m above. Turn left along this and follow it above the hill fence to the point where you crossed it on the ascent. Continue down the lane back to the start.

WALK 11
Cwm Cynwyn Valley

Start	Pont Caniedydd (SN039 244)
Map required	Central Map OL11
Distance	8.75km (5.6 miles)
Total ascent	350m (1150ft)

A short valley walk in picturesque Cwm Cynwyn but be prepared to get wet feet! After crossing a small stream, the first half of the route follows the little-explored eastern side of the valley. A short steep climb to the Gap (Bwlch ar y Fan) brings you to the Roman Road. This allows fast progress back to the start but do not forget to savour the wonderful atmosphere of this glacial valley as you tread in the footsteps of Roman soldiers. Route finding in a wide valley is always variable but safe and providing you can locate the Gap in bad weather there are few difficulties. The main features of the walk are a nature reserve, the glacial nature of the valley, the views from Cribyn and the Roman Road.

From the start at Pont Caniedydd, cross the bridge and head south up the road, passing **Bailea Farm** on the way. On the right of the road in the valley of Cwm Sere is a woodland nature reserve (see Walk 7) and at the head of this valley is the north-east face of Pen y Fan. To its left is Bryn Teg ridge. Ignore the turning on the left to Bailea Farm and follow the road up the hill to where it swings sharp left and through a gate. Ignore this turning and follow the stony track straight ahead to a gate in the hill fence on the far side of which is a National Trust sign for Cwm Cynwyn. This stony track is popularly known as the Roman Road.

There is nothing specifically Roman about this road, but it is extremely likely to be of Roman origin as the fortress at Y Gaer is near the mouth of this valley and the road would have been the natural link with other fortresses to the south at Pen y Darren, Gelligaer and Cardiff.

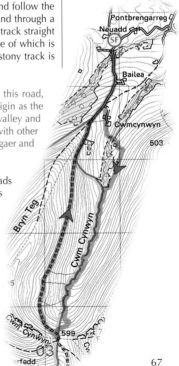

Fifty metres on the left is a gate which leads into a walled enclosure at the end of which is a second gate. Follow through these and down the rough track to another gate and so to the farm (New Cwmcynwyn) via the lane to the right. Pass through the farmyard to a gate and through this to a stony lane where ahead is a fine view of Fan y Big. At the bottom of this stony lane the track bears to the right up the valley. Ignore this and continue dropping down left alongside the green moss-covered stone wall to the stream.

Cross the river, aiming for the gate opposite. In spate, this river may be very

Old Cwmcynwyn farm

difficult to cross. If so, retrace to the stony lane south of New Cwmcynwyn Farm and continue up the right side of the stream, rejoining the route at the stone sheep pens.

Keep left up the hill to the top and round to the right into the grounds of Old Cwmcynwyn Farm.

From the ruins turn left by the wire fence and up the track to a stile and so to the path running along the hillside 50m above. Turn right (SSW), following the path towards the head of the valley. The hill fence turns right and drops down to the river bed.

Continue along the east side of the valley above the stream down to the right. Eventually the indistinct path you are following meets the stream bed at a hawthorn tree and old stone enclosures (hafodydd). Leave the stream course here and strike up left onto the lower reaches of Fan y Big on which there is a double row of small rock outcrops which should be passed on the left-hand side. Traverse right above the lower outcrops and climb steadily to the **Roman Road**. ◀

You will want to catch your breath after this sustained climb and there are plenty of interesting features to see from this good viewpoint.

Turn left at the Roman Road and make your way to Bwlch ar y Fan, the 'Gap between the Peaks'. This is an ideal place to appreciate the almost perfect U-shape of this glacial valley (see 'Glacial origins of U-shaped valleys,' Introduction).

From here head northwards back down the western side of **Cwm Cynwyn** to the hill fence. Follow the stony track, the Roman Road, and then the road back to the start.

WALK 12
Cwm Oergwm and Cefn Cyff

Start	Pen-yr-heol (SN058 240)
Map required	Central Map OL11
Distance	9.75km (6 miles)
Total ascent	436m (1430ft)

The walk follows the western side of Cwm Oergwm through fields and some woodland to emerge onto open hillside at the hill fence. From here it drops to the stream below to a scenic waterfall and then up the stream course to the head of the valley. The headwall is climbed by a steep ascent to the lowest point of the ridge which is then followed north-west to Fan y Big. A long, gentle descent along Cefn Cyff brings the walk to an end. Following the stream provides easy route finding and the ascent of the headwall is straightforward but steep and the alternative route ascending to Craig Cwareli is even more strenuous. The flowers and birdlife in the valley are extremely varied and complement the waterfall and mountain scenery.

Start at the holiday cottages (Pen-yr-heol) just past the houses of **Rhiwiau** and Llyn Fron. Leave the yard in front of the cottages on your right and follow the waymarked path into the field in front of the pens. After 100m it rejoins the track.

The deciduous woodland a little way down on the opposite side of the valley hides two **Iron Age hill forts**, Coed y Brenin and Coed y Caerau. The woodland occupying the valley floor is owned and managed by the Brecknock Wildlife Trust (see Walk 13).

IRON AGE HILL FORTS

The poorly preserved defences of the almost rectangular Coed y Brenin Hill Fort are situated in Coed y Brenin overlooking the entrance to Cwm Oergwm. It is marked on the map as a 'homestead'. Natural protection is afforded by deep stream gullies on the east and west and by the slope dropping away north-west, but the fort is vulnerable to the south-east where the slope rises steeply.

Just to the east of the 'homestead' is a 'settlement' – Coed y Caerau Hill Fort. This is another Iron Age hill fort, again naturally protected by stream gullies on either side but overlooked by ground rising steeply to the south-west. The highest fortifications face uphill to defend this weakest point and are well preserved. Charcoal debris has been found inside the ramparts on a level, oval platform. Other platforms have been discovered in nearby woodland and these are ancient charcoal-burning hearths.

Waterfall, Cwm Oergwm

Continue for 200m and cross a stile. The route follows a clearly defined, slightly sunken track between mainly hawthorn, alder and ash. Coming to a gate there is a good view into **Cwm Oergwm**. From here follow the overgrown track between trees, with an old stone wall on the left, to a

gate and a stream bed. Below, on the left, are the remains of buildings but the track continues and divides 200m further on near a metal store for sheep fodder.

Leave this hut on your right and after twenty paces take the track down to the left and continue along the upper edge of deciduous forestry and into woodland. This part of the route is difficult to follow as there is no obvious path and care in route finding must be taken after the feed store is reached.

Once in the woodland, head straight towards **Cwm Cwareli** to a gate in a stone wall. Beyond is open hillside and from here navigation is straightforward. Drop down left to the stream bed and proceed upstream to a waterfall. You will find secluded waterfalls and perhaps a heron hunting for fish. Buzzards are often found soaring on thermals overhead. Further on you come across a picturesque waterfall. ▶

The alternative route to Craig Cwmoergwm via Craig Cwareli leaves from here.

To continue on the main route scramble upstream from the main fall, encountering many smaller waterfalls on the way to the head of the valley. Towards the head of the valley the stream has cut into mounds of glacial moraine left behind after the last Ice Age. From the base of the headwall climb steeply to the lowest point of **Craig Cwmoergwm** (SN038 199).

This small **col** on the ridge is easily identified by piles of Brownstones and a number of dry-stone structures including a bothi built by the army. This is an unsightly affair as the roof is made of polythene and there is much discarded rubbish – the majority of which is easily identifiable as being of military origin.

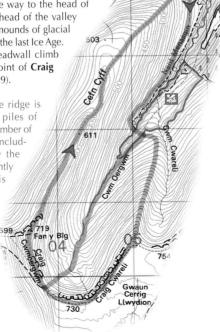

71

Craig Cwareli from Fan y Big

Fan y Big is easily
identifiable by a
distinctive sandstone
block protruding on
the north-west side.

From the col turn right (NNW) and gently climb along
the eroded path to the summit of **Fan y Big.** There are fine
views looking westwards to Cribyn and Pen y Fan. ◄

Descend (NNE) along **Cefn Cyff** (see Walk 10) along
a distinct path to a prominent cairn made of Brownstones.
Continue (NNE) along the ridge path which is now quite
wide. Keep to the path along the top of the ridge to some
old quarry spoils where a distinctive track to the left of these
descends the end of the ridge. A good reference point to aim
for is the church tower at Llanfrynach if you miss this track.
The old quarry track winds its way downslope to a gate in
the hill fence. Pass through this and follow a stony track bordered on either side by stone walls with hazel, birch and
holly back to the start.

Alternative route
Follow the directions above to the waterfall. Climb
south-east to the spur which separates the side valley of
Cwm Cwareli from Cwm Oergwm. The ridge high above
is gained by a steep strenuous ascent of this spur and
might well require crampons and an ice axe in winter
conditions.

Turn right (SSW) along **Craig Cwareli** and around **Craig Cwmoergwm** to the col marked by piles of Brownstones. The crags below have an interesting flora (see Walk 14). Rejoin Walk 12 on the ridge.

WALK 13
Cwm Oergwm and Gist Wen

Start	Near Tregaer Farm (SN072 250)
Map required	Central Map OL11
Distance	13.75km (8.4 miles)
Total ascent	540m (1818ft)

The route follows the eastern side of Cwm Oergwm through woods and fields to a waterfall. The valley bottom is followed to the headwall and a steep ascent is required to gain the col. The level ridge is followed around the eastern sides of Cwm Oergwm and Cwm Cwareli back to the start. Route finding is straightforward and the highest peaks are avoided so that only low mist would require recourse to the map. The walk is not over-strenuous but provides a great deal of interest, ranging from wetland flora and birdlife to glacial scenery and two hill forts. The eastern ridge of Cwm Oergwm provides some of the finest panoramic views in the Beacons.

Start near the entrance to **Tregaer Farm**. Walk south-south-west along the road and after 150m another track on the right leads to Tregaer Farm. Ignore this track. There is a fine view of Cwm Sere and Pen y Fan to the south-west from the gate here. Continue along the road for a further 950m, passing Caerau Farm on the left. After another 50m there is a sign on the right side of the road which indicates a footpath 150yds ahead.

Directly opposite the modern bungalow (Cwm Oergwm Isaf) on the right is a stile with a right of way leading down to the stream. Do not take this. Up on the hillside to the south-east are two archaeological sites – a homestead and settlement (see 'Iron Age hill forts,' Walk 12). Unfortunately, there does not appear to be a public right of way to these.

View west from Rhiw Bwlch y Ddywallt of Cwm Cwareli and Cwm Oergwm

The route continues along the road to a gate and the start of a bridleway. Pass through the gate and follow the bridleway surfaced in coarse limestone chippings but which soon changes to a muddy track.

Look out for an old ruin at SN058 228 that was probably once used for making charcoal. In this area you may see heron, raven, meadow pipit, skylark, buzzard, duck, finch and robin.

A gate leads to dense coniferous forestry for 300m before passing through a second gate and into more open hillside. Leave the sheep pens on the left and follow a marked path

CWM OERGWM WOODLAND

The narrow strip of deciduous woodland found in Cwm Oergwm is similar in character to that found in Cwm Sere and is likewise managed by the Brecknock Wildlife Trust. The nature reserve comprises some 20 acres of deciduous woodland extending for almost 1.5km along the steep eastern bank of Nant Menasgin. The valley bottom is wet and the species that grow here reflect these boggy conditions. Species found in these swampy conditions include trees such as alder and wetland plants such as great horsetail, kingcups and broad-leaved cotton-grass, the latter found in more open calcareous flushes. This reserve is also blessed with woodland birds typical of the north-eastern valleys. You may well see redstarts, pied flycatchers and buzzards.

through land owned by the National Trust. After 1km the hill fence is reached. Pass through a gate and turn right following a ditch alongside the fence to the stream below. Cross over using a few stones and follow the eastern bank to a waterfall.

Nant Menasgin tumbles over a number of small waterfalls created by more resistant bands of sandstone but is a 'misfit' in this valley. This is because the classic U-shape was carved by glacier ice and not scoured away by the stream (see 'Glacial Origins of U-shaped valleys,' Introduction). Look out for birds such as dippers and wagtails darting low over the water and, if you are very quiet, you may well be able to watch a heron stalking fish. Buzzards are often found soaring on thermals overhead.

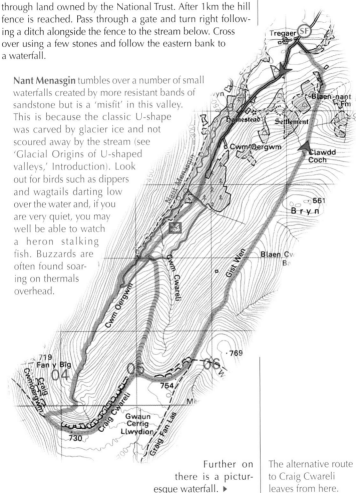

Further on there is a picturesque waterfall. ▶

The alternative route to Craig Cwareli leaves from here.

Continue following the stream to the head of the valley. Towards the head of the valley the stream has cut into mounds of glacial moraine left behind after the last Ice Age. The ruddy-brown crags high up to the left and right are formed by resistant bands of Brownstones (see 'Geology of the Brecon Beacons,' Introduction).

Climb steeply to the right to the lowest point of **Craig Cwmoergwm** (SN038 199). This small col is easily identified by piles of Brownstones and a number of dry-stone structures including a bothi built by the army. Shelter can be found here for a well-earned rest, snack and warm drink, especially if the weather is inclement.

The disused sandstone quarries on Bryn were once worked for local building stone.

Turn left (SE) and follow the ridge path around the head of the valley to **Craig Cwareli** and on to Bwlch y Ddwyallt, Rhiw Bwlch y Ddwyallt and **Gist Wen**. Follow the obvious path, Ffordd Las or Bwlch Main, passing below the rounded summit of **Bryn** on your right. ◄

Continue along the well-worn path descending Rhiw and **Clawdd Coch**, which then passes along the fence above Coed Tyle-du. Make sure you do not stray too far to the right and inadvertently reach the wrong gate in the hill fence. Once the fence above Coed Tyle-du drops to the left, make for the gate and stile in the hill fence just to the right of Coed Cae-rebol.

Standing on the ridge at the head of Cwm Oergwm

Drop through the clearing, with denser woodland on the left and sparser woodland on the right, and then swing to the right to a gate in the corner of the field. Leave the farm of Tir

Hir on the right and follow the track which swings down to the left along a line of trees, cross the ford and follow the farm lane back to the start.

Alternative route
Follow the main route to the hill fence. Strike south and ascend the spur of land which separates the side valley of **Cwm Cwareli** from Cwm Oergwm. This is an exciting and strenuous route and may well require crampons and ice axe in winter conditions. Below to the left is the glacial cirque of Cwm Cwareli. The disused stone pens are hafodydd or sheep pens (see Walk 8). The steep inaccessible crags on the eastern side of the valley are an interesting arctic-alpine habitat (see Walk 14). Rejoin the main route at the start of Bwlch y Ddwyallt.

WALK 14
Cwm Oergwm Ridge

Start	Near Tregaer Farm (SN072 250)
Map required	Central Map OL11
Distance	15km (9.3 miles)
Total ascent	566m (1857ft)

This route follows the last two ridges of the north-eastern valleys. A fairly easy ascent brings you to Bryn, from where you have one of the finest panoramic views in South Wales. After careful attention to the route in the early part of the valley, following the ridges is not difficult but be prepared and capable of using a map and compass if the weather closes in on the higher sections. Height is gained and lost without undue exertion. The inclined geology of the Beacons can be appreciated fully from the eastern aspect and some of the finest views in the area are to be found.

Start at a stile opposite the entrance to **Tregaer Farm** where a track leaves the road to the south-east. The stile is signed to Rhiw Bwlch y Ddwyallt. Follow this track south-east, climbing gently for a while, and then drop into a wooded gully and

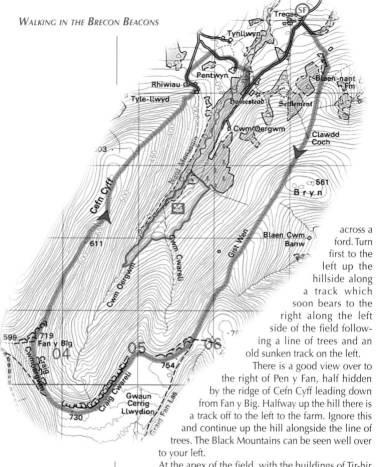

across a ford. Turn first to the left up the hillside along a track which soon bears to the right along the left side of the field following a line of trees and an old sunken track on the left.

There is a good view over to the right of Pen y Fan, half hidden by the ridge of Cefn Cyff leading down from Fan y Big. Halfway up the hill there is a track off to the left to the farm. Ignore this and continue up the hill alongside the line of trees. The Black Mountains can be seen well over to your left.

At the apex of the field, with the buildings of Tir-hir Farm on your left, turn right to a gate and then left up the hill. The path winds through widely spaced small oak trees diagonally right up the slope to a more open area. Head straight up the hill, with the boundary of deciduous woodland of Coed Cae-rebol on your right, to the hill fence. This is crossed by a stile and the route joins a farm track rising from the left. The wall on the right swings further away to the right and the path steepens as it climbs the hillside to **Clawdd Coch.** There are good views here of Pen y Fan, Cribyn and Fan y Big. The woodlands of Coed y Caerau and Coed y Brenin down to your right contain two Iron Age hill forts (see Walk 12).

The path skirts to the right of the summit of **Bryn**, reaching a somewhat flatter section. On the opposite side of the valley is Cefn Cyff which leads down from the summit of Fan y Big. Make a mental note here that this will be your descent route. Due east from this point you can look down into the valley of Cwm Banw. ▸

The deciduous woodland in the valley floor is a woodland nature reserve (see Walk 13).

From here climb along Ffordd Las which ascends first **Gist Wen** and then Rhiw Bwlch y Ddwyallt, meeting a junction of paths ascending from Carn Pica and Graig Fan Las. Continue round the spectacular ridge which swings around the head of **Cwm Cwareli** and **Cwm Oergwm**.

The path is eroded and route finding is simple, but care must be taken in icy conditions or in strong winds as the route has precipitous drops immediately on the right.

Craig Cwareli and the flat 'lunar landscape' of Gwaun Cerrig Llwydion provide some of the best locations for views of the Beacons' highest summits. The dip slopes of the Plateau Beds which cap Corn Du and Pen y Fan clearly parallel each other from these viewpoints. The bedding of the underlying Brownstones exposed in the faces of Cribyn and Fan y Big are also in step.

Craig Cwareli, Bwlch y Ddywallt and Craig Fan-las have an interesting flora. Steep crags below the ridge path are inaccessible to grazing sheep in places and have some interesting species. Rock stonecrop (*Sedum forsteranum*), mossy saxifrage (*Saxifraga hypnoides*), purple saxifrage (*Saxifraga oppositifolia*), and limestone bedstraw (*Galium sterneri*) have been recorded here.

Just around the head of Cwm Oergwm, the broad path drops into a small col, well marked by a military bothi. From the col, climb (NNW) to the summit of **Fan y Big.** From here there are magnificent views of Cribyn and Pen y Fan. The summit has a block of sandstone protruding from its western side.

The Beacons summits from Fan y Big

Coppicing is a traditional woodland practice which involves harvesting wood from a tree by cutting it down just above the ground, leaving just a stump from which new growth develops.

The field is improved grassland used to fatten ewes just after they have given birth in spring.

Descend almost due north from the summit on an obvious path along **Cefn Cyff** (see Walk 10) to old quarry spoils where you will meet and descend a quarry track to the left of these. The old track winds its way downslope to a small copse and a gate and stile in the hill fence marked by a blue bridleway indicator. Walk down the stony lane to a gate leading to Pen-yr-heol, the beginning of a road.

Turn left past the white-washed cottage of Llwyn Fron on the right. Shortly the road swings down to the right with a lane leading to **Rhiwiau Farm** on the left. Round the corner there are some coppiced beech trees about 50m further on the left-hand side. ◄

Take the first gate on the right, signposted with a yellow National Park Authority sign and a sign to Llanfrynach. A path waymarked by two arrowed posts crosses the field to a stagger in the hedge. The right of way marked on the map follows the right side of the hedge but in fact the waymarked route passes through the gate keeping the hedge on the right. Look back the way you have just come for one of the last views you will have of the summit of Pen y Fan. ◄

Follow the track curving to the right to a gate and a road. Turn right at the road, avoiding the temptation to cross it on the National Park waymarked route. Drop down the hill.

As the road bears to the right, and on the apex of the bend before reaching the farm, there is a bridleway on the left. Take the path (bordered by hedges of blackberry and wild rose) down to a stile and the river **Nant Menasgin**.

Cross over the stone bridge, turn left then right up the waymarked track. Follow the conspicuous track which winds first left, then diagonally right, up the hillside. The woodland here has an understorey of hazel with the odd oak, ash, holly, birch, beech, hawthorn and blackthorn.

The sunken path leads up on the edge of a field between two banks lined with mature trees. A stile is reached and a gate with a National Park Authority sign with a blue arrow indicating a bridleway up to the right. Cross over the stile and turn left (NE) down the lane with a new bungalow on your right. Continue past the farm on your right and follow the tarmac lane back to the start near Tregaer Farm.

WALK 15
Cwm Oergwm Valley

Start	Near Tregaer Farm (SN072 250)
Map required	Central Map OL11
Distance	5km (3.2 miles)
Total ascent	200m (328ft)

A low-level route in Cwm Oergwm taking the eastern side of the valley to a waterfall and returning along the western valley side. Once beyond the hill fence feel free to choose how you explore this delightfully quiet area with minimal exertion. The wildlife and the history of this valley provide more than enough interest. Since this is a valley, gradients are easy but route finding is slightly difficult through the fields and woods on the western side of this classic U-shaped glacial valley. This area is particularly interesting because of its woodland and bird nature reserve.

Start near the entrance to **Tregaer Farm**. Walk south-south-west along the road and after 150m another track on the right

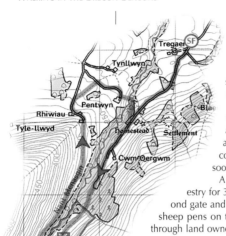

leads to Tregaer Farm. Ignore this track. Continue along the road for a further 950m, passing Caerau Farm on the left. After another 50m there is a sign on the right side of the road which indicates a footpath 150yds ahead.

The route continues along the road to a gate and the start of a bridleway. Pass through the gate and follow the bridleway surfaced in coarse limestone chippings but which soon changes to a muddy track.

A gate leads to dense coniferous forestry for 300m before passing through a second gate and into more open hillside. Leave the sheep pens on the left and follow a marked path through land owned by the National Trust. After 1km the hill fence is reached. Pass through a gate and turn right following a ditch alongside the fence to the stream, **Nant Menasgin**, below. Cross over using a few stones and follow the eastern bank to a picturesque waterfall (SN050 219).

Climb out of the stream bed, to the west, to a stone wall (the hill fence) with a stream gully running parallel to it and to a gate. Pass through the gate and follow a path through woodland and then along the edge of deciduous forestry, eventually climbing diagonally to the left towards a metal feed store.

Leave this to your left and continue to a gate and a stream gully. Below to the right are the remains of old buildings. The path climbs gently from here, following an overgrown track lined by remnants of a dry-stone wall. Pass through the gate at the top and follow a slightly sunken path to sheep pens, beyond which is a metal road. The old path is blocked by a gate some distance before the farm buildings but the route makes a detour into the field below, skirts below the sheep dip, passes through a gate and so to the road.

Shortly the road swings down to the right, with a lane leading to **Rhiwiau Farm** on the left. Take the first gate on the right, signposted with a yellow National Park Authority sign and a sign to Llanfrynach. A path waymarked by two

arrowed posts crosses the field to a stagger in the hedge. The right of way marked on the map follows the right side of the hedge but in fact the waymarked route passes through the gate keeping the hedge on the right.

Follow the track curving to the right to a gate and a road. Turn right at the road, avoiding the temptation to cross it on the National Park waymarked route. Drop down the hill. As the road bears to the right, and on the apex of the bend before reaching the farm, there is a bridleway on the left. Take the path down to a stile and the river.

Cross over the stone river bridge, turn left then right up the waymarked track. Follow the conspicuous track which winds first left, then diagonally right, up the hillside.

The sunken path leads up on the edge of a field between two banks lined with mature trees. A stile is reached and a gate with a National Park Authority sign with a blue arrow indicating a bridleway up to the right. Cross over the stile and turn left (NE) down the lane with a new bungalow on your right. Continue past the farm on your right and follow the tarmac lane back to the start near Tregaer Farm.

Looking north-east over the lower reaches of Cwm Oergwm to the Black Mountains in the distance

2 EASTERN VALLEYS AND RIDGES

The Beacons summits from Craig Cwmoergwm

WALK 16

Bryn

Start	Pencelli Church (SN087 245)
Map required	Central Map OL11
Distance	6.25km (3.6 miles)
Total ascent	386m (1266ft)

A varied walk with the initial stages passing through farm land followed by an excursion onto hill land to one of the best viewpoints in the Beacons. The circular route then winds its way through picturesque woodland with photogenic views of the River Usk and the Black Mountains beyond. The beginning and end of the walk require care in path finding but height gained is moderate, making the route safe and fairly gentle. The main interest lies in the exceptional view from Pen y Bryn and in the solitude of the approaches.

Start at the end of the road where it widens at **Pencelli Church**. Straight ahead is a tarmac track with the church on the right. On the left is a bridleway which is the end of the return route. Take the track to the left of the church and after a few metres bear left off the tarmac track and onto a rough path. ▶

    Pass in front of the house ahead, leaving it to your left, and follow a yellow National Park arrow which directs you down to the stream and over a wooden bridge. Follow the path up the slope and bear right through a gap in the line of trees ahead. Look for a gate in the hedge on the right and go through this, turning left onto the tarmac road and on up the hill. At the crest of the hill take the track off to the right which is marked by a National Park sign.

The church is surrounded by yew trees, a species traditionally found in churchyards and, in early spring, snowdrops can be found at the side of the church.

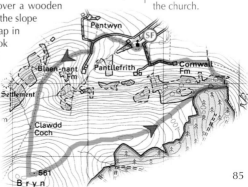

85

The Brecon Beacons from Clawdd Coch

Pass through the gate and along a track between hazel trees. Look back for a superb view of the Black Mountains. Cross over a stile and continue towards conspicuous **Scots pines**. Just past these is a good view of the north face of Pen y Fan (WSW). Continue up the field on the right of the track and after 200m cut into the track on the left and over the stile at the side of the gate.

Once over the stile in the hill fence, keep close to the fence on the right. When this drops down to the right, head straight up left to the summit of **Bryn**. ◄

Red grouse are thought to breed in this area.

The rounded, pool-covered summit of Bryn is a superb vantage point for views and photographs, especially of the northern ridges and summits of the Brecon Beacons. Looking west, the first ridge is Cefn Cyff leading to Fan y Big, the middle ridge is Bryn Teg leading to Cribyn and the final ridge is Cefn Cwm Llwch. To the north-west can be seen Llyn Syfaddan and the rolling wave-like front of the Black Mountains.

At the summit turn north-east to a new cairn and head down left of the coniferous forestry with a bearing (060°) slightly to the right of Llangorse Lake which you can see in the distance. Keep the coniferous forestry on the right and follow the track down the ridge. The track then cuts back to the left towards deciduous woodland, meeting this at a wall. Turn right along the wall and climb the stile into the wood.

Once in the wood, follow the path down **Allt Feigan.**
The path curves round to the right through oak and beech
wood. Follow the track along the left of the wall, which is
now broken down, and on to a gate and stile. Ignore the path
that leads straight ahead and swing left down the hill. The
wood is on the left and looking right over the fields there is
a wonderful view of the River Usk meandering in the valley
floor, with the Black Mountains beyond.

The track continues north-west along the northern edge
of the wood to a gate and on to a second gate at the beginning of a wide track.

Turn left through the second gate and along the stony track
but be careful not to miss this turn as it is easy to continue on
down the hill. Follow the track and pass through the farmyard
at **Cornwall Farm**. Stay on the bridleway, cross a small ford and
turn right following the bridleway down the hill to the church.

Pencelli Church

WALK 17

Cwm Tarthwynni Circuit

Start	Talybont Reservoir car park (SN100 197)
Map required	Central Map OL11
Distance	7.5km (5 miles); with extension 11.5km (7.5 miles)
Total ascent	570m (1850ft); no added ascent with extension

A fairly strenuous walk involving a continuous ascent of 480m (1500ft) over the first 2.5km. A short walk to a col is followed by an airy ascent up a narrow rib to the southern end of Craig y Fan. From this vantage point a panorama unfolds of the beautiful valley below and of the mountains to the east. A worthwhile extension to the route around Waun Rydd provides superb views of the summits, ridges and valleys of the Brecon Beacons. Most of the route is easy to follow but you may need to rely on compass bearings as the high plateau is reached. Expect to be challenged by the length of the walk and the stiff pull on some of the ascents. In addition to the quality of the views, you visit a Bronze Age funerary mound and see something of 19th-century intervention in reservoir and railway construction.

Leave the car park, cross the road and go through a double gate. Walk up this road for about 50m to a stile on the right. Leave the road here and follow a grassy track between two fences with the stream of **Nant Tarthwynni** down in the

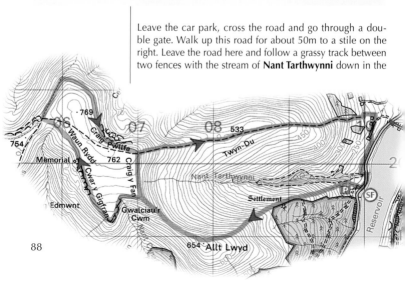

valley to the right. Straight up the valley you can see Carn Pica, the large cairn on the top of the summit.

Climb this grassy track, with rushes (*Juncus*) on either side, to another gate and stile. Crossing over this reach a steep field with stone walls on both sides and the coniferous forestry plantation up to the left. ▶

Walk up this field keeping close to the wall on the right until it drops steeply to the right. From this corner cut up across the slope to the end of the coniferous forestry where there is a gate in the far corner of the field (SN088 194).

Walking up the valley there is a good view of the cliff at the end (Craig y Fan) with the stream running straight into its head. Looking back down the slope you can see the head of the Talybont Reservoir and beyond to the main ridges of the Black Mountains.

The slopes of the valley are mainly covered in bracken with some deciduous woodland dotted around on the lower slopes.

Two **settlements** are marked on the Ordnance Survey map and these were once Iron Age hill forts which may have formed part of a settlement complex. The northern perimeters of both forts lie in the field you are crossing but the majority is in coniferous forestry plantation which has damaged and obscured most of this archaeological site.

TALYBONT RESERVOIR

This is the largest reservoir in the Beacons and serves the Newport area. It was completed in 1938, flooding the valley and affecting 25 farms and 2875 acres of land, which was a compulsory purchase. Land around the reservoir was included and subsequently leased to the Forestry Commission. The creation of the reservoir made the surrounding hillside less viable for agriculture and the comparative fertility of the 'bottom land' was reduced. Without it the higher rougher pasture cannot support stock. Forestry was favoured by the Water Authorities as it was thought not to be a pollution threat to water supplies in the same way as livestock. The area was created as a Local Nature Reserve in 1975 in recognition of its ornithological importance and, in particular, as a wintering area for migrant birds. The reserve covers 490 acres and was set up by the National Park Authority through an agreement with the Welsh Water Authority and the Forestry Commission. It is managed by the Brecknock Wildlife Trust.

From the gate and stile in the hill fence, make straight to the summit of **Allt Lwyd** ahead of you (bearing 235°). Just

Looking southwards along the ridge of Gwalciau'r Cwm

to the right are the col and the ridge which leads up to Craig y Fan.

Vegetation on the rounded summit of Allt Lwyd is dominated by hare's tail grass (*Eriophorum vaginatum*), heath rush (*Juncus squarrosus*) and bilberry (*Vaccinium myrtillus*). Localised patches of ling (*Calluna*) occur as well as common cotton-grass (*Eriophorum angustifolium*) and wavy hair grass (*Deschampsia flexuosa*).

Cross north-west over to the col and ascend the steep prow to the top of the ridge, the last bit of ascent to gain the high Beacons plateau. Surprisingly, the face to the right is at a much shallower angle than it appeared from the approach walk. It is made up of erosion-resistant Brownstones which form the spectacular crags to the west and, if you look carefully in this direction, you can just see the two highest summits in South Wales, Pen y Fan and Corn Du (see Walk 21).

The extended walk around Waun Rydd leaves from here. To continue on the main route turn north following the head of this valley along **Craig y Fan**. From here there is a good view down the valley, with deciduous woodland at the bottom, Tor y Foel in the middle ground and the distinctive shape of the Sugar Loaf mountain in the distance. Look out for the interesting shapes created by the eroding peat hags on the plateau area of Waun Rydd (see 'Peat haggs,' Walk 20). Waun Rydd is covered mainly in hare's tail grass (*Eriophorum vaginatum*) together with common cotton-grass (*Eriophorum angustifolium*), heath rush (*Juncus squarrosus*) and scattered bilberry (*Vaccinium myrtillus*), mat grass (*Nardus*) and crowberry (*Empetrum nigrum*).

The top of the crag leads you to a distinctive landmark, **Carn Pica**, a large cairn made of sandstone.

Carn Pica is a modern cairn marking the site of a **Bronze Age funerary mound**. Pottery urns containing the remains of human cremations were placed in an excavated pit covered by large flat stones. A cairn was then built on the site. Radio-Carbon dating methods have given an early Bronze Age origin around 2200–1400BC for these sites in the Beacons.

From the cairn, descend the obvious eroded path E down a steep slope to the col and climb slightly to an area covered in bilberry with a little heather, **Twyn Du**, on the north

Carn Pica

91

side of the valley. Halfway along this ridge you meet a rutted track – follow this down. This turns into a wide grassy track which drops down the side of the hill to the left (N) of the ridge and through a boggy area. Just to the left of this is the corner of the fence and an old dry-stone wall. Keeping the wall on your left, follow the grassy track down the hillside to a gate and a stile. If you miss the track, head straight for the reservoir dam and the stile is easily found as the fences on either side funnel you to it. From here the path becomes obvious again.

The path follows a gully carrying a stream on the right. Follow this downslope and, after a few hundred metres, cut across the stream to the right-hand bank. You are now on a raised bank with ditches on either side with a field on the right. Cross the small stream which joins from the right and continue to a gate on the right.

Through the gate and immediately on the left is a barn. Continue straight ahead towards a house called Berthlwyd-fach. The route follows the field below the house. Turn left after the cattle grid through a gate, head for the fence at the bottom of the garden. Walk across the slope to a stile in the hedge.

The route drops to the bottom left-hand corner of the field to a very old track lined with hazel and the odd oak tree. Pass through a gate and along a line of coppiced hazel trees parallel with the road. Go through another gate and along the track. In the next field drop to a gate where there is a stream and a series of old tank traps. Turn right at the road, cross over the bridge and walk a short distance back to the car park on the left.

Extension

Turn left (W) along the top of the crags around the head of **Gwalciau'r Cwm** to the end of **Cwar y Gigfran**. From the southern end of Cwar y Gigfran the valley of Blaen-y-glyn and Blaen Caerfanell comes into full view. This is a glacial hanging valley with the stream plunging in a series of waterfalls into the valley below.

Follow the top of the crags (NNW) and continue on this bearing, passing through eroding peat haggs (see Walk 20) to Rhiw Bwlch y Ddwyallt, the ridge above Cwm Oergwm. The inaccessible crags below provide an unusual plant habitat (see Walk 14).

The views from the ridge of **Rhiw Bwlch y Ddwyallt** are some of the finest in the Beacons and really capture the essence of the area. The valley immediately below is Cwm Cwareli. It has been deeply cut by the stream which later joins with Nant Menasgin in Cwm Oergwm.

Turn right (NNE) along the obvious path and when it begins to drop contour around to the right (E). Gradually, the slope above Cwm Banw (the valley to the north) becomes steeper until it forms the steep slopes of **Craig Pwllfa**.

The glacial cirque below is the most sheltered area from the sun's rays in the whole valley and so was most susceptible to freeze-thaw action. The resulting moraine, known as a **nivation ridge**, is now bisected by a stream (see Walk 25).

Continue contouring the top of these to Carn Pica where you pick up the main route once more.

WALK 18
Blaen-y-glyn and Allt Forgan

Start	Pont Blaen-y-glyn Forestry Commission car park (SN064 169)
Map required	Central Map OL11
Distance	9.25km (6 miles)
Total ascent	490m (1607ft)

This route combines the beautiful waterfall scenery of Blaen-y-glyn with a classic view of the Brecon Beacons' highest peaks. The walk gains height by following the course of the Caerfanell which plunges in a series of waterfalls. This now popular area is soon left behind as the route enters the glacial hanging valley of Cerrig Edmwnt. Finally, the ascent along the mountain stream of Blaen-y-glyn brings you to one of the finest vantage points in the whole of the Central Beacons. ▸

The return route follows the eastern valley ridge and drops to the satellite peak of Allt Forgan before the final descent back to the start. Route finding is simple as long as the river is followed but care should be taken as you climb up to the high ridges. A compass and map are needed along with the skills to use them. The walk is quite long and strenuous and the main points of interest are the waterfalls, the superb mountain views and the war memorial to a crashed bomber.

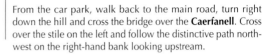

From the car park, walk back to the main road, turn right down the hill and cross the bridge over the **Caerfanell**. Cross over the stile on the left and follow the distinctive path north-west on the right-hand bank looking upstream.

This path passes through mainly alder and hazel with some hawthorn, bramble and the odd birch. The river is the Caerfanell and its initial stages are quite wide as the water tumbles over a boulder-strewn bed. Keep glancing at the stream bed for a specialist bird of this habitat, the dipper. On a quiet day you are likely to chase a pair upstream for a certain distance until they reach the end of their territory. At this point they will either hide or make a quick dash back downstream. Their companions, yellow and pied wagtails, are also abundant here. The woodland on your right is composed of alder because the area is very wet and is fed by a number of springs issuing from the hillside above. Alder thrives in wet ground conditions and is characteristically found in boggy areas and along watercourses. The best time to explore this area is early in the morning when the woodland is full of bird song.

The riverbed soon changes character as the stream course narrows and you will come across a small **waterfall** which has a man-made rim and the water then tumbles over a natural exposure of Brownstones. At this point the damp alder wood is left behind and the slope up to the right is mainly covered in bracken with a prominent large oak tree. The banks of the stream are still lined with alder.

The stream is soon forced to run in a very narrow chute and just above this, beyond a right-hand bend in the stream, there is the first glimpse of the largest fall in the lowest section of the valley. Just after the bend in the river is a confluence of streams and the first of the main waterfalls is encountered just after a wooden bridge crosses the stream. The fall can be explored by crossing the bridge and proceeding up the left bank.

After exploring the fall, rejoin the path which continues above the gorge on the right side of the stream. Looking back down the river the high ground in front of you is Pant y Creigiau and below this is the line of the **old railway** cutting through the forestry.

BRECON AND MERTHYR JUNCTION RAILWAY

A continuous break in the forestry on the eastern side of the Talybont Valley is not a firebreak but the course of the old Brecon and Merthyr Junction Railway. This was opened in January 1863 and tackled some very steep gradients, only to close a century later in 1962. The narrow-gauge line (4ft 8½in) carried coal from Merthyr to Brecon, as well as lime for agricultural purposes, made from limestone removed from extensive quarries between Pontsticill and Dowlais. The return trains hauled pitwood and other timber, cattle, sheep and pigs, cereals, beer and cider. The most difficult engineering task was the construction of a 666yd tunnel at Torpantau through the ridge separating Glyn Collwn from Taf Fechan. Excavation began in March 1860 from both sides of the ridge, with nine men in action, night and day, at each end of the tunnel bore. The final 'break through' was achieved on 11 January 1862 and, amazingly, the two centres coincided within two inches.

Continue following the path along the stream valley which, after a short distance, straightens to give good views of the mountains ahead. In front is the slope of **Cerrig Edmwnt** which leads up to the southern end of Cwar y Gigfran. On the right-hand side, in the near foreground, the valley sides are covered in oak and alder. Continue up the path to the stile in the hill fence near to the stream.

There is an unusually large stone block immediately on your right above the hill fence which has been carefully inscribed with the initials G.H. and the date 1845. The initials may well be those of the Gwynne Halfords of Buckland, a large landowning family in Victorian times (see Walk 8 where a similar stone is described on the wall of a sheep pen).

The view north of the glacial hanging valley of Cwm Edmwt from Allt Forgan

The path now works high above the stream which flows in a steep-sided wooded gorge. At the end of the gorge is the last waterfall in this section. The path comes close to this and it is worth making a short detour to stand at the top of the fall and look back down the gorge.

From the fall the route keeps close to the stream passing a ruin where there is a good exposure of sandstone. Continue along the stream and follow the right fork (N) up towards the head of the valley. It is easier to climb up the left side of the stream gully where there appears to have once been a man-made cutting, possibly associated with the disused quarry. The spoils of this can clearly be seen above to the right below the line of Cwar y Gigfran.

Finally, you join the main path and ridge of **Rhiw Bwlch y Ddwyallt**. Your long climb is rewarded with a breathtaking view of the north-eastern valleys and ridges. The valley below is Cwm Cwareli which joins the classic U-shaped Cwm Oergwm. To the west (103°) are the three highest summits of the Beacons. Cribyn lies in front of Pen y Fan with

Corn Du to the left, separated from the major summit by a small col. To the north is a green and yellow patchwork of fields and the town of Brecon. This scene is particularly dramatic if there has been a light snowfall, as this picks out the relief in the steep faces of the mountains (see 'Geology of the Brecon Beacons,' Introduction).

Turn east and contour south-south-east along a path which winds its way through the peat haggs. Continue to the war memorial just below the crest-line at SN062 200.

This is a memorial to the crew of a **Wellington bomber** which served with 214 Squadron in 1941, taking part in raids on Hamburg and Rotterdam. Tragically, the plane crashed while undertaking a training exercise. It is likely that the mountain was covered in cloud with the pilot flying low trying to pinpoint his position. Each Armistice Day, wreaths of poppies are placed on the memorial which is close to the remains of the crashed aircraft itself.

From here, climb to the end of the crags and walk (SSE) along **Cwar y Gigfran** to where it turns sharply north. The slopes below Cwar y Gigfran have a hummocky topography characteristic of landsliding. Here the rock and soil are slumping, due to gravity, on curved slippage planes. This has resulted in backward tilting of upper bedding plane surfaces. You will just be able to see the summits of Pen y Fan and Corn Du over the headwall of the valley to the west from the end of Cwar y Gigfran. ▶

Notice how well cleaved the Brownstones are in the cliffs here, making them break apart very easily to expose their bright red surfaces.

The ridge is a fine vantage point affording views to the south of the hidden valley of Blaen-y-glyn and of the Talybont Valley and its reservoir (see 'Talybont Reservoir,' Walk 17). To the west are the limestone escarpments of Mynydd Llangynidr and Mynydd Llangattock.

One can truly appreciate from this high point the scale of the decimation of this area by the **coniferous forestry plantations**. During the winter months the larch loses its greenery and it is then clear that it is often planted on the edges and as linear tracts within the forestry. The reason for this is that larch is less combustible and so acts as a firebreak.

Looking down Cwm Cynafon from the southern end of Cwar y Gigfran

Descend the steep slope S to the col where you will notice a conspicuous furrow dropping straight down the slope. This was once used to transport stone down from the quarry. Head for a gate in the hill fence ahead where a dry-stone wall drops away from it. Keeping above the boggy area, go through the gate and strike up left to the summit of **Allt Forgan**.

This is a fine viewpoint for the ridges on the western side of the Talybont Valley. The vegetation here is largely purple moor grass (*Molinia*) together with ling (*Calluna*) and crowberry (*Vaccinium myrtillus*). Looking back up Blaen-y-glyn

HANGING VALLEY

The upper half of Blaen-y-glyn has been left 'hanging' above the main Talybont Valley. During the Ice Age, Blaen-y-glyn would have contained a small glacier which fed the main glacier responsible for carving out the Talybont Valley (see 'Glacial origins of U-shaped valleys,' Introduction). This glacier in turn fed one of the major glaciers of the Beacons which flowed down the Usk Valley. The stream which now drains the classically ice sculpted U-shaped hanging valley has cut a small 'V' notch in the valley floor. The stream plunges over the 'overhang' in a series of waterfalls.

you have one of the best views of the glacial hanging valley. Look out for buzzards wheeling overhead.

From the summit descend due west to pick up the line of the dry-stone wall. Cut down the zigzag path (W) to where a stream gully drops to the right. On a clear day you will be able to see some **stone ruins** down to the right which is where you will pick up a track. If you cannot see these follow the gully downslope, keeping to the right-hand fork, and after passing the third large alder, turn left and pass above a group of silver birch. Continue diagonally downslope to some stone ruins and pick up a track here which leads back to the main waterfall. Retrace the path along the bank of the river to the road bridge. Turn right up the road and back to the Forestry Commission car park.

> The Forestry Commission car park at Torpantau is an alternative starting point for the upper parts of Walk 18 and Walk 19. It is useful for those not wishing to include the waterfalls in their route, making for shorter walks, but still with the opportunity of reaching the high Beacons' plateau. This is the highest road pass in the Brecon Beacons and is a good starting point for quick ascents to the high ridges.

Alternative starting point
Torpantau Forestry Commission Car Park (SN056 176)

The upper parts of Walk 18 and Walk 19 can be followed by joining them in the upper half of the valley. This can be reached from the Torpantau car park by continuing (NNE) along the forestry track. Turn left up a forestry ride and then right at a T-junction, finally coming to a stile in the hill fence (SN059 182). Cross over the stile and strike (NNE) across the hillside to meet the stream above the last area of deciduous woodland and the last waterfall. This is where you join Walk 18 and Walk 19.

WALK 19
Blaen-y-glyn and Craig y Fan Ddu

Start	Pont Blaen-y-glyn Forestry Commission car park (SN064 169)
Map required	Central Map OL11
Distance	10km (6 miles)
Total ascent	490m (1608ft)

This route is similar in character to Walk 18 but returns along the western side of Blaen-y-glyn and then follows another stream with a spectacular waterfall hidden in dense coniferous forestry. Numerous alternatives can be followed, bringing great variety to the length and character of the walks. This is a part of the Brecon Beacons which can satisfy all interests and abilities. The route can be followed easily along the river bed but ability to read a map is needed in the higher reaches. The whole walk is moderately strenuous but this is rewarded by the waterfalls, some of the finest views in the Central Beacons and spectacular glacial features.

From the car park, walk back to the main road, turn right down the hill and cross the bridge over the **Caerfanell**. Cross over the stile on the left and follow the distinctive path north-west on the right-hand bank looking upstream.

The stream is soon forced to run in a very narrow chute and just above this, beyond a right-hand bend in the stream, there is a first glimpse of the largest fall in the lowest section of the valley. Just after the bend in the river is a confluence of streams and the first of the waterfalls is encountered just after a wooden bridge crosses the stream. The fall can be explored by crossing the bridge and making your way up the left bank.

After exploring the fall, rejoin the path which continues above the gorge on the right side of the stream. Continue following the path along the stream valley which, after a short distance, straightens to give good views of the mountains ahead. Continue up the path to the stile in the hill fence near to the stream. The path now works high above the stream which flows in a steep-sided wooded gorge. At the end of the gorge is the last waterfall in this section. The path comes close to this and it is worth making a short detour to stand at the top of the fall and look back down the gorge.

Follow the stream past the waterfalls, taking the the right fork (N) where it divides, and continue all the way up the valley to the ridge of Rhiw Bwlch y Ddwyallt and the junction of four paths at SN058 206.

The extended walk to around Craig Cwareli leaves from here. To continue on the main route turn left (SSW bearing 200°) and follow the path along the edge of **Graig Fan Las** and cross the stream of **Blaen Caerfanell** at 050 192 where it disappears over the cliff edge to fall to the valley below.

Looking back along Craig Fan Las the peat haggs of Waun Rydd take on a surreal appearance in the low afternoon light. The area to the right is Gwaun Cerrig Llwydion, also composed of eroding peat haggs (see Walk 20). Carefully inspect the exposed surfaces of Brownstone blocks

The Caerfanell stream plunges over a number of waterfalls, marking the step in the hanging valley, Blaen-y-glyn

101

for evidence of ripple marks. Particularly good examples can be found on rock surfaces where the path crosses the stream which then tumbles over cliffs to the valley below. These ripples were formed in the beds of streams during the Devonian period of geological time (see Walk 21).

GWAUN CERRIG LLWYDION

The flat lunar-like landscape of Gwaun Cerrig Llwydion and the ridge of Craig Cwareli provide some of the best locations for views of the Beacon's highest summits. From these viewpoints, the dip slopes of the Plateau Beds (which cap Corn Du and Pen y Fan) and the bedding of the underlying Brownstones (exposed in the faces of Fan y Big, Cribyn and Pen y Fan) align (see 'Geology of the Brecon Beacons,' Introduction). Peat hags interspersed with areas of frost-shattered Brownstones provide plenty of foreground interest and this horizontal plateau helps to balance the tilt of the Beacons ridges (see 'Peat haggs,' Walk 20). These rock fragments were produced by freezing and thawing at the end of the last Ice Age and have recently been exposed by erosion of the peat cover which developed in post-glacial times on poorly drained, flattish areas. This area is covered in badly eroding blanket mire which results in islands of peat being stranded amongst peaty channels or stone. Their tops are covered in hare's tail grass and common cotton-grass (*E. angustifolium*), together with occurrences of bilberry, heath rush (*Juncus squarrosus*), wavy hair grass (*Deschampsia flexuosa*) and deer grass (*Trichophorum cespitosum*).

From this ridge the Mumbles Lighthouse can be seen on a clear day to the south-west, the sea sometimes glowing a deep red in a setting winter sun.

◀ Keep to the edge which now turns south-south-east (bearing 152°) along **Craig y Fan Ddu**. The obvious path tends to cut across to the right but following the crag line is more interesting, even though the path is not so obvious. Descend the steep prow of the mountain (S) to the edge of the forestry (SN055 179). The path is wide here and has suffered from erosion. The exposed soil can be very slippery in wet conditions.

The dense **coniferous woodland** which can be seen growing in the Blaen-y-glyn valley is managed by the Forestry Commission. The plantation here dates from the late 1950s and originally consisted of Norway spruce. Much of this has now been replaced by Sitka spruce, and Japanese larch (*Larix leptolepis*) is now planted instead of larch (*Larix europaeo*). The whole of the

Talybont Valley has been heavily planted, shattering the ambience of a wild, natural mountain environment.

From the corner of the forestry, continue on the path which now follows the stream-way of **Nant Bwrefwr** to the entrance of a Forestry Commission car park. The steep banks of the small stream gorge are covered mainly in hazel, ash, alder and birch. Be careful not to miss a number of surprisingly high waterfalls to your right.

Do not cross the cattle grid into the car park (Talybont–Torpantau) but keep following the left bank of the stream, past three small waterfalls, and cross the river above the last of these. The path goes down the right side of the stream through dense larch woodland for about 100m to the top of a large **waterfall**. Cross back to the left bank above this and continue between conifers along a path. Eventually you are forced away from the bank of the stream but be careful not to miss the largest fall which has to be explored by dropping down a steep slope and then walking back up the river bed for a little way. Continue downstream along a path which follows the left bank and arrives at a track and a bridge along which you turn right and so back to the start.

Frost-shattered Brownstones on Gwaun Cerrig Llwydion

103

Waterfall in Blaen-y-glyn

Extension

From the ridge of Rhiw Bwlch y Ddwyallt at the head of Blaen-y-glyn follow the northern facing crag line around the head of Cwm Cwareli along Bwlch y Ddwyallt. Continue along **Craig Cwareli** until its direction changes to the west. Cut across **Gwaun Cerrig Llwydion** (bearing 128°) to where the Blaen Caerfanell stream cuts the southern end of Graig Fan Las and disappears over the cliff edge to fall to the valley below. Rejoin the main route here.

Alternative route
Waterfall walk combined with a circuit of the head of the valley

Follow the main route to the top of the **waterfalls**, where the gradient becomes gentler and the forestry has been left behind. Leave the stream course near where a small tributary joins on the right and a wall meets the main stream on the left. Head north-east, guided by a straight furrow in the hillside, and climb to the southern end of **Cwar y Gigfran**.

This furrow was once used for transporting stone from the quarry above and to the right. The summits of Pen y Fan and Corn Du are just visible over the headwall of the valley to the west from the end of Cwar y Gigfran. Notice how well cleaved the Brownstones (see Walk 18) are in the cliffs here, making them break apart very easily to expose their red surfaces.

Follow the crag line (NW) to rejoin Walk 19.

Alternative route
Low-level waterfall walk

Follow the main route to the top of the **waterfalls.** Cross the stream just above the last fall and walk south to a gate in the hill fence around the coniferous forestry plantation. This is being logged and replanted, so the forest roads are continuously changing in character. It is possible to find your way to the Forestry Commission car park where you join Walk 19.

WALK 20
Torpantau Circuit

Start	Torpantau Forestry Commission car park (SN056 176)
Map required	Central Map OL11
Distance	13km (8.5 miles)
Total ascent	354m (1160ft)

An initial short steep climb to Craig y Fan Ddu is all that is needed to reach the high Beacons plateau and a spectacular upland walk. The route follows the ridge around the head of Blaen-y-glyn and then around another ridge which forms the head of Cwm Oergwm. From the summit of Fan y Big, the route drops to the Gap and a circuit of Torpantau brings you back to the start. The initial ascent is strenuous but once the ridge is gained the day's hard work is complete. Even in poor visibility, the route can be followed easily by keeping to the ridges, but compass bearings may be needed at the highest point. The geomorphology of the Beacons can best be seen from this walk and the viewpoints are spectacular.

Walk out of the car park, recrossing the cattle grid, and climb immediately right up the path on the right-hand bank of **Nant Bwrefwr** stream with the coniferous forestry plantation on the right. Numerous plant-rich flushes can be found along the banks of Nant Bwrefwr. Interesting species include bog pimpernel (*Anagallis tenella*), lesser valerian (*Valeriana dioica*) and marsh arrow-grass (*Triglochin palustris*).

At the corner of the forestry the path leaves the stream and heads directly up the wide eroded path for the southern end of **Craig y Fan Ddu.** From this viewpoint the decimation of the Talybont Valley by conifer plantations is fully visible.

CONIFEROUS FORESTRY

Conifers that are planted tightly together on hillsides throughout the National Park are alien to this area, having been imported for commercial reasons. They have been planted closely together to produce what is called a 'close canopy' so that

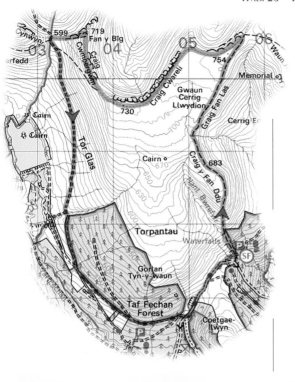

they produce straight stems with a minimum of branching. This technique has a disastrous effect on wildlife in that it entirely suppresses both growth on the forest floor and also any natural regeneration. There is a total absence of ground-flora, partly due to the intense shade and partly due to the carpet of conifer needle-leaves which produce an acidic surface layer. The humic acid produced from the breakdown of the needles contaminates streams and lakes and, if the receiving waters cannot 'buffer' this acidic solution, fish and other life will die, resulting in a sterile environment. The trees are all of the same age and are 'clear-felled' at maturity, leaving the areas prone to soil erosion and leaching. The end result is an area whose top-soil is sterile, since no fertile leaf mould has been produced, or with no top-soil where this has been washed away after felling.

Keep to the eastern edge of Craig y Fan Ddu and follow the line of crags north to where the small stream of **Blaen Caerfanell** cuts the path and disappears over the cliff edge to fall to the valley below. Cross the stream and continue along **Graig Fan Las** (NNE) to a junction of paths on Rhiw Bwlch y Ddwyallt. Notice the classic U-shape of the hanging valley (see Walk 18).

PEAT HAGGS

These islands of peat are all that remain of a once continuous cover which has been eroded by water-cut channels. Peat is formed in boggy conditions when dead plant material accumulates. The process began in this area around 6000 years ago and continued for about 4000 years. The present climate is drier and this may account for the absence of peat formation in this area today. Man has not contributed to this decay by peat cutting at this site, but grazing animals have had a detrimental effect. Peat erosion has been further accelerated by excessive drying due to the wind and the sun and by the action of rain, frost, ice and snow. The cusp-shaped margins of the peat haggs provide essential shelter from the elements for sheep. Eventually, this striking topographical feature will unfortunately disappear completely.

The Sugar Loaf and Craig y Cilau

Turn left (SW) and follow the ridges of Bwlch Ddwyallt and **Craig Cwareli** to the col where there is a bothi. Continue following the ridge path along Craig Cwmoergwm to the summit of **Fan y Big**. The path is eroded and route finding is simple, but care must be taken in icy conditions or in strong winds as the route has precipitous drops immediately on the right.

There are fine views as you walk to the summit of Fan y Big looking westwards to Cribyn and Pen y Fan. Fan y Big is easily identifiable by a distinctive sandstone block protruding on the north-west side. The steep scarp faces of these ridges and summits are formed from resistant Brownstones (see 'Geology of the Brecon Beacons' Introduction).

Descend west to **the Gap** (Bwlch ar y Fan). Down below in the head of this U-shaped valley is an interesting glacial feature (see 'Head of Cwm Cynwyn,' Walk 8; 'Glacial origin of U-shaped valleys,' Introduction). Up above to the west is the impressive crag of Craig Cwm Cynwyn (see Walk 10).

Turn left and take the Roman Road south across the slopes of **Tor Glas**. Do not turn right on the track descending to the lower reservoir but stay on the track which skirts the lower edge of the forestry on your left. You may well be walking in the footsteps of Roman legionnaires (see Walk 11).

When the track meets the road at SN035 174 continue along the edge of the forestry on a Forestry Commission ride which contours around the base of **Torpantau** and eventually meets the Pontsticill to Talybont road. Here you will see signs of the **old railway line** (see Walk 18) which ran from Pontsticill to Talybont. Walk north-east along the road back to the car park.

3 SOUTH-WESTERN VALLEYS AND RIDGES

Cantref Reservoir

WALK 21
Neuadd Horseshoe

Start	Taf Fechan Forestry Commission car park (SN036 171)
Map required	Central Map OL11
Distance	12.5km (7.6 miles)
Total ascent	650m (2132ft)

This is the most popular circular walk in the Beacons, taking in the three highest peaks in South Wales – Cribyn, Pen y Fan and Corn Du. The route is reasonably strenuous and the time required to complete it deceptively long. Route finding, however, is straightforward. This is a classic walk worth doing on quieter days. The most difficult sections are the initial climb to the ridge and the ascents of the main peaks. It is difficult to exaggerate the beauty of the views from this walk and the varied geology of the area can be well appreciated.

From the car park, head north along the road to the Lower Neuadd reservoir. Enter the reservoir grounds through the main gate, where there is a Welsh Water sign, and cut down left to a bridge. Cross this and climb up to the reservoir dam, crossing this to a gate in the fence and so to the open hillside.

From the dam you have the first opportunity to make a mental note of the route ahead. Up to the left is the ridge which leads to Corn Du and Pen y Fan. The route then drops to the col and climbs steeply to the summit of Cribyn before dropping to another col and returning via the Roman Road (see Walk 11). An extension climbs to Fan y Big and contours above Tor Glas before following a gully back down to the reservoir to complete the horseshoe. ▶

Climb steeply left alongside the forestry fence and so up to the ridge above. There is a good view during the ascent, looking up the valley with Graig Fan Ddu to the left. Notice that the hillslope leading up to **Graig Fan Ddu** has a pronounced step. This is a well developed antiplanation terrace, a post-glacial feature (see Walk 4).

The Lower Neuadd reservoir has been drained for some time and rhododendrons have now taken over the bed on the left-hand side.

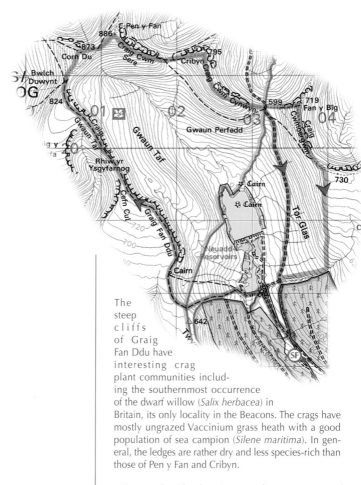

The steep cliffs of Graig Fan Ddu have interesting crag plant communities including the southernmost occurrence of the dwarf willow (*Salix herbacea*) in Britain, its only locality in the Beacons. The crags have mostly ungrazed Vaccinium grass heath with a good population of sea campion (*Silene maritima*). In general, the ledges are rather dry and less species-rich than those of Pen y Fan and Cribyn.

Once on the ridge there is a magnificent view west to the Carmarthen Fan, to the Rhigos and the heads of the valleys. To the east are the Neuadd Valley and the headwaters of the Taf Fechan. South is the Taf Fechan reservoir. Back in the direction you have just walked is the distinctive shape of the Sugar Loaf near Abergavenny. North, through Bwlch ar y Fan where the Roman Road passes, you can see the Black Mountains.

Continue north along the ridge to a point above the northern tip of the Upper Neuadd reservoir. Across the valley is the Roman Road coming up from the Neuadd reservoirs and crossing over the gap between Fan y Big and Cribyn and so on to Brecon. ▶

The track continues along the crest of the ridge close to the steep drop on the right and care should be taken in winter. Towards its northern end the ridge falls off to the west and becomes the headwall to Cwm Crew.

The rocks that make up the ridge you are walking on are the **Plateau Beds** and these are well exposed in the northern crags of Cwm Crew. These have been eroded where the path drops to the col at Bwlch Duwynt but remnants are still left as distinctive flat caps to the summits of Corn Du and Pen y Fan.

At the end of the ridge descend to the col at **Bwlch Duwynt** where the track from the left comes up from Pont ar Daf. Ascending Corn Du brings you up the rock steps to the summit plateau. This is best crossed at its western edge and so to the summit cairn. The rocky steps up to the flat

The descent from Graig Fan Ddu

On a clear day Mumbles Bay can be seen looking left (SW) down the Neath Valley, as can the lighthouse on Mumbles Head and the smoke rising from the stacks of Baglan Bay.

113

Corn Du and Pen y Fan from Craig Gwaun Taf

topped summit of **Corn Du** are formed by a resistant cap of Plateau Beds. Corn Du is the best vantage point for views west of Fforest Fawr (see Walk 28) and Bannau Sir Gaer, otherwise known as the Carmarthen Fan. Beyond the cairn is a superb view down the steep northern face into Cwm Llwch (see Walk 2).

The path which skirts below to the right of Corn Du can be taken if weather conditions deteriorate. This rejoins the route at the col before Pen y Fan.

Now strike east, by a flattened cairn, and descend to the col and the well worn track up to the summit of **Pen y Fan**. This col can be heavily corniced in winter and it is advisable to keep well back from the edge. From the summit cairn of Pen y Fan, leave at the southern end of the plateau on a well-worn artificially stepped path. The path swings round to the east and drops steeply at first to the col.

Pen y Fan is the highest point in South Wales and, on a clear day, provides one of the finest vistas in Britain (see 'Pen y Fan vista,' Walk 1). As you descend **Craig Cwm Sere**, look to your left for a fine view of the north-east face of Pen y Fan. The National Trust, which owns this land, has carried out extensive path restoration here. Keep to the made-up path to prevent further erosion problems.

The col is a natural place to stop and learn of the geological history of the northern Brecon Beacons ('see Earth Movements,' Introduction). Looking north down Cwm Sere you can see a perfect example of a glacial U-shaped valley (see Introduction).

Ascend **Cribyn** steeply to another cairn. Then descend following the path along **Craig Cwm Cynwyn**, which swings first south and then east down to the gap and the Roman Road. Stop at the gap and take in some of the interesting features in this area. To the north is the head of Cwm Cynwyn and up to the left is Craig Cwm Cynwyn (see Walk 10). You may well be resting where Roman legionnaires once marched (see Walk 11). Down below in the head of this U-shaped valley is an interesting glacial feature (see 'Head of Cwm Cynwyn,' Walk 8).

The extended route via Fan y Big and Craig Cwmoergwm starts from here. To continue on the main route turn right (S) and follow the Roman Road across **Tor Glas**. When you come to the stream gully at the southern end of the Lower Neuadd reservoir, do not drop down the gully to the right but cross the gully and continue along the track along the edge of the forestry to the road. Continue (S) down the road back to the start.

Extension

For those who still feel energetic, climb **Fan y Big** from the Roman Road. Fan y Big is easily identifiable by a distinctive sandstone block protruding on the north-west side. The steep scarp faces of these ridges and summits are formed from resistant Brownstones (see 'Geology of the Brecon Beacons,' Introduction).

From the summit, turn due south and follow the ridge path along **Craig Cwmoergwm** to the military bothi at the low point of the ridge. Below to the north is Cwm Oergwm, the last of the north-eastern glacial U-shaped valleys.

Leave the main ridge path just past here and contour south along the top of the slope of Tor Glas. When you meet a stream gully (**Nant y Gloesydd**), just before the Forestry Commission plantation, descend following the right bank to the Roman Road and rejoin the main route.

WALK 22

Cwm Llysiog and Waun Wen

Start	Lay-by by Pont Nant Gwinau (SN008 128)
Map required	Central Map OL11
Distance	8.75km (5.2 miles)
Total ascent	220m (720ft)

A short walk based on Cwm Llysiog, a valley which has a bleak, isolated atmosphere, due to it probably being the least visited of all the valleys in the Central Beacons. This feeling of solitude is really the only appeal of this walk as the access to the valley is via a monotonous climb through coniferous forestry with the return route crossing open moorland of little interest. The head of the valley has a number of picturesque waterfalls. No great height is reached so the walk is not strenuous, but there are sections requiring very careful route finding in bad weather. The main features of interest are the waterfalls.

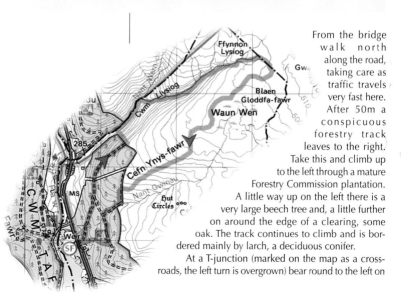

From the bridge walk north along the road, taking care as traffic travels very fast here. After 50m a conspicuous forestry track leaves to the right. Take this and climb up to the left through a mature Forestry Commission plantation. A little way up on the left there is a very large beech tree and, a little further on around the edge of a clearing, some oak. The track continues to climb and is bordered mainly by larch, a deciduous conifer.

At a T-junction (marked on the map as a crossroads, the left turn is overgrown) bear round to the left on

The secluded valley of Cwm Llysiog

a gravel road and after a short distance you come to clearings on both sides, the one to the left giving a clear view of the road and the river beyond, the **Taf Fawr**. Carry straight on, the forestry on the left has been felled leaving good views down to the Taf Valley. This gravel-covered track terminates in a turning area, but carry straight on along an overgrown track covered in Juncus. Some 100m later cross the hill fence via a gate.

The path emerges almost on top of the hillside, above the valley below on the left. There is a fine view directly into **Nant Wern-ddu**. Just along from the gate in the hill fence there is a good view of the lower reaches of Cwm Llysiog and the upper reaches of Nant Wern-ddu. Drop straight down to your left (NW) into the bottom of Nant Wern-ddu.

The lower reaches of the valley are totally blanketed with conifers but there are some deciduous trees lining the stream bed. Further up the valley there are a few scattered trees on the sides and adjacent to the stream. The river bed is wide and boulder strewn with a few diamond-shaped gravel bars. Reed-moss (*Juncus effusus-Sphagnum recurvum*) flushes are widespread along the stream. In the valley bottom, near Y Fforch, there are some collapsed dry-stone buildings (possibly

117

hafodydd, see Walk 8), with a path marked on the map leading to them. The lower areas of the valley sides are covered in patchy bracken and above this are mat grass (*Nardus*) and heath rush (*Juncus squarrosus*).

Just after the derelict stone buildings, take the right fork of the river into **Cwm Llysiog**. Shortly, the sides become much steeper and it is easier to follow the left bank which is not quite so severe.

This area is quite attractive. The valley sides are dotted with birch and hawthorn with the stream tumbling over boulders and down a bedding plane for a few tens of metres. On the right are Old Red Sandstone exposures with red marls below. These are interbedded with thinner units of sandstone, with rowan growing out of them (see 'Geology of the Brecon Beacons,' Introduction).

Look out for flattened rushes and large amounts of rock debris brought down by small rivulets on either side of the stream, evidence of the Jeckyl and Hyde character of this valley. Notice the steamcourse runs perpendicular to the dip of the rocks and this is known as a strike stream. It is not a coincidence that the best rock exposures are found along the south-western bank as the erosive power of the water is concentrated in the down-dip direction, causing the stream to migrate sideways. Towards the upper reaches of this valley the stream bed narrows and twists between interlocking spurs.

Skylark

FLASH FLOODS

Nant Wern-ddu has a reputation for producing flash floods and a number of measures have been taken in the past to combat this danger. A large stone embankment was constructed in the 1950s in the lower reaches of the valley in order to divert and slow down flood waters. A dam was also built halfway up the valley at around the same time. The reason for this valley being prone to flash floods is that it is a 'strike' valley since it lies at right-angles to the south-south-easterly dip of the rocks. You will notice from the map that there are more streams on its north-western bank (where the rocks dip towards it) than on the south-western sides where the rocks dip away from the stream. These tributaries drain an extensive upland area which rapidly supplies relatively large quantities of water to a small valley with a straight watercourse. These are ideal ingredients for flash floods.

Continue to an area of deciduous trees lining outcrops of Brownstones on the right of the stream (marked on map). Just upstream is a small fall, about 3m high. The crags to the left are covered in ivy and numerous species of moss and ferns.

The valley splits again just after this fall. The smaller tributary on the left is well worth exploring with two small falls in a narrow gorge. The banks are covered in heather (*Calluna*), bilberry (*Vaccinium myrtillus*), mosses, ferns and lichens. Return to the confluence and follow the right-hand tributary to an impressive fall (3–4m high), with another a little further on. Both these falls are formed by thick beds of resistant sandstone, the first of Plateau Beds and the second of Grey Grits (see 'Geology of the Brecon Beacons,' Introduction). Climb up to the left of these falls.

From this vantage point there is a fine view looking back, the valley in the foreground having interlocking spurs with the larger valley beyond being more U-shaped. A spring, Ffynnon Lysiog, flows from the base of the Grey Grits along the banks of the last northern tributary which meets the main streamway between the last two falls. At this point the stream is covered in a film of orange iron hydroxide precipitated by bacteria. The waters issuing from the spring further up the tributary are rich in iron and have a reputation for their healing properties.

Just above the falls, the stream disseminates into flat open moorland, an expanse of bog with eroded peat haggs, dominated by purple moor grass (*Molinia*), with hare's tail grass (*Eriphorum vaginatum*) and deer grass (*Trichophorum cespitosum*) in places. The ridge along the southern side of the valley is the line of a geological fault which lies along the northern boundary of the Neath Disturbance. The rocks to the south have been down-thrown just enough to bring the Plateau Beds into direct contact with the Brownstones.

Up to the north is the flat area of Waun Lysiog and the slope above is Twyn Mwyalchod. To the north-east the line of coniferous forestry is part of the large Taf Fechan Forest, an extensive Forestry Commission plantation in the next valley.

From immediately above the waterfall walk south-south-east (bearing 150°) across Twyn y Groes. This is a wet area of purple moor grass (*Molinia*). Shortly (after about 500m) you meet and turn right (SW) onto two parallel drainage ditches,

Derelict Stone Buidings in Cwm Llysiog

about 10m apart and marked on the map as a track. These meander south-westwards across **Waun Wen,** a large featureless area where there are patches of common cotton-grass (*Erica tetralix*) and heather (*Calluna*) amongst purple moor grass. This open moor is quite a challenge from a route finding point of view and, with a covering of snow, navigation has to be done purely by compass as these ditches are lost from sight. The ditches become indistinct for short stretches but eventually appear to be double, parallel tracks, periodically marked by concrete fence posts, with barbed wire wrapped around them.

Gradually lose height crossing this moor and the coniferous forestry you walked through on the way up eventually becomes visible. The route crosses a rivulet by a bridge of railway sleepers. Straight ahead a gate leads into the coniferous forestry. Pass through this and turn left after a short distance, along a wide forest track to **Nant Gwinau**. The track swings right, following the bank to a T-junction with a well-used forestry track.

Turn left (S) and cross over the stream to the next clearing on the right marked by a dry-stone wall. Across on the opposite side of the valley is Garwnant Forest Centre. This junction is marked on the map as a crossroads but the track on the left is obscured when approaching from this direction and the track on the right is overgrown. Turn right and follow the stone wall down the hillside to the stream. Continue along the bank down to the bridge and the lay-by.

WALK 23
Cwm Crew and Cefn Crew

Start	Corner of Forestry Commission plantation off A470 (SN993 173)
Map required	Central Map OL11
Distance	7.5km (4.8 miles); with extension 10.9km (6.8 miles)
Total ascent	420m (1500ft); with extension 503m (1772ft)

This is an interesting walk centred on Cwm Crew, a valley with an isolated feel even though it is adjacent to the busiest area of the Brecon Beacons National Park. Access is not easy and perhaps for this reason it is a very quiet and secluded area. From various vantage points during the walk a great deal of the surrounding countryside can be viewed and the route can easily be extended to take in Corn Du and Pen y Fan, the highest summits in South Wales. The geological history of Cwm Crew is interesting and there are fine views from the top of the valley.

The logical start for a walk in Cwm Crew would be to leave the road just to the left or right of the Nant Crew Bridge and follow the banks of the stream up the valley. There is room to park at SN993 163, a lay-by at the north-east end of Cantref reservoir just north of the road bridge. Unfortunately, you have to cross 350m of private land to gain access to National Trust land and at the present time there is no permitted access.

It is worth stopping at Nant Crew Bridge for the fine view into the valley. A large oak stands guard over the entrance to Cwm Crew. On a windless day the adjacent pool reflects the image of the tree but these conditions are few and far between as the prevailing winds are south-westerly and are funnelled up the valley. The depth of the pool is governed by the water level in Cantref reservoir and in a particularly dry year the pool disappears, leaving the gravel stream bed exposed.

From Nant Crew Bridge go north along the A470 to the start at 993 173. Go through a gate in the hill fence and onto National Trust land. Ascend the hillside on the

View from the road bridge into the entrance to Cwm Crew

north of the fence and over the brow of the hill. Drop down to the valley bottom, picking up a distinctive sheep track just above the stream.

Looking up the valley, keep to the left (NW) side passing numerous hawthorn trees. After a short distance, drop down past these and follow the river bed itself. There are two sheep hafodydd (see Walk 8) at 004 187. A path rises up above the river bed just after these, necessitating the crossing of numerous side valleys as they drop steeply to the river.

Continue past more stone hafodydd and just after these drop down to the stream bed to a small waterfall with a rowan tree. Keep in the river bed and examine small cliffs with unusual mosses and ferns on them. Below the next fall is a willow and the highest fall has to be bypassed on the right. In high winds, the funnelling effect of the valley can cause the water to be blown vertically into the air in a large 'spout'.

Keep close to the river above the fall and aim for the end of a 'tongue' of moraine which divides the streamcourse into two where the valley narrows before it changes direction to the north and becomes Blaen Crew. The tributary to the right soon disappears in a boggy area.

Climb up the prow of the moraine and continue diagonally up to the right to **Rhiw yr Ysgyfarnog**. Turn along the ridge (NNW) to **Craig Gwaun Taf** at the head of Cwm Crew.

From Rhiw yr Ysgyfarnog look back across the valley you have just ascended. Notice another **moraine rib** which runs down the slope from the southern end of Craig y Byllfa. Both this moraine and the lateral moraine you have just walked along were formed at the end of the last Ice Age when a lingering block of ice survived in the most shaded area of Cwm Crew. Rock debris from the steep slopes above the ice tobogganed down its slippery slope and accumulated around its edge.

The upland area around Cwm Crew, together with a very narrow strip along Rhiw yr Ysgyfarnog, and the ridge south, still has its protective resistant cap of Plateau Beds (see 'Geology of the Brecon Beacons,' Introduction). From the ridge you have excellent views of the Beacons summits. The peak on the left (due north) is Corn Du, followed by Pen y Fan, Cribyn and Fan y Big to the east. Blaen Crew very nearly became part of the Taf Fechan Valley during the Ice Age, and all that separates them today is Rhiw yr Ysgyfarnog. The Taf Fechan (Little Taf) Valley below is the catchment area for the Neuadd reservoirs.

CWM CREW

This is a very secluded valley since difficult access dissuades most walkers. Unfortunately, it has not entirely escaped the alien intrusion of coniferous forestry on the slopes near the mouth of the valley. Once these are left behind the valley has a truly wild feel, with hawthorn and birch scattered around, but in the upper reaches these disappear giving a barren appearance.

For much of its length, Nant Crew is confined to a 15m wide straight channel within which it meanders. The dip of the rocks is to the south-south-east which has resulted in the northern and western valley sides eroding faster than the more stable southern and eastern sides where the rocks dip into the hillside. A few hafodydd are found on the valley floor; these derelict stone-walled pens were once used when sheep flocks were moved to higher ground in the summer. Upstream from these pens the stream changes character, becoming ever smaller, and the watercourse is forced to twist its way around interlocking spurs of land. The stream bed now consists of exposed red sandstone bedrock instead of boulders and gravel. Small waterfalls and pools are found where the confined stream tumbles over more resistant bands of Brownstone. Here you will find interesting rock exposures of micaceous red sandstone, particularly on the right (SE) bank.

The valley changes character when it becomes narrower and swings around to the north.

Cwm Crew is a classic U-shaped valley indicating that it was cut by a glacier. Much of the sides and floor are covered in unconsolidated sediments of glacial and periglacial origin. This 'head' moved downslope over the permanently frozen subsoil during periglacial conditions which existed after the main Ice Age. The stream left in the valley then began to cut a sharp 'V' down through these deposits, resulting in the abrupt change of slope on either side of the stream. In places, the stream has washed away all these superficial deposits exposing Old Red Sandstone bedrock underneath. Waterfalls result when the stream encounters a more resistant band of sandstone.

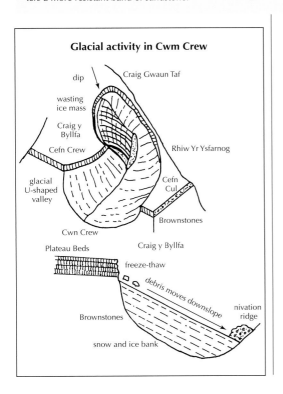

Glacial activity in Cwm Crew

dip

Craig Gwaun Taf

wasting ice mass

Craig y Byllfa

Cefn Crew

Rhiw Yr Ysfarnog

glacial U-shaped valley

Cefn Cul

Brownstones

Cwn Crew

Craig y Byllfa

Plateau Beds

freeze-thaw

debris moves downslope

nivation ridge

Brownstones

snow and ice bank

Looking down Cwm Crew from Craig y Byllfa

The extended walk to Pen y Fan leaves from here. To continue the main route turn west and follow the ridge of **Craig y Byllfa** which curves around to the south. The crags of Craig y Byllfa are an impressive sight and are steep enough for snow to avalanche in winter. A detached block of Plateau Beds at the head of the valley is slowly creeping downhill, leaving a well-developed landslip scar.

Keep to the high ground and follow the eastern side of **Cefn Crew** (SW) to where the ridge ends. Lose height steadily by dropping down the prow of the mountain towards the forestry and make your way down to the gate in the hill fence at the road.

Extension

A worthwhile extension to the route is to visit the two highest summits in South Wales.

Continue (NNE) along **Craig Gwaun Taf** and sweep around north to **Bwlch Duwynt** (Windy Gap), which certainly lives up to its name. Ahead of you is a well-worn path leading up to the flat-topped summit of **Corn Du**. From the summit descend (E) to the col and then climb gently to the top of **Pen y Fan**.

The resistant **Plateau Beds** which cap Corn Du and Pen y Fan have been eroded away on the intervening ridge which is composed of softer Brownstones. The ridge is eroding at a faster rate than the summits and this is a good example of differential erosion.

Retrace your steps to the col but do not climb back up to Corn Du. Instead, follow the distinctive path which skirts along Corn Du back to Bwlch Duwynt. Follow the ridge back to the head of Blaen Crew and rejoin the main route where you began your excursion to the high summits.

Snowdrops

Craig Cerrig-gliesad

4 FFOREST FAWR

WALK 24
Craig Cerrig-gleisiad

Start	Lay-by off A470 (SN971 222)
Map required	Central Map OL11
Distance	3.3km (2 miles)
Total ascent	280m (918ft)

A short walk packed full of interest. The route passes through the hollow of a periglacial cwm, overshadowed by steep craggy cliffs which are the habitat of rare alpine and arctic-alpine plants. This area is part of a National Nature Reserve and must be respected as such. There is a relatively short but steep ascent and the main features of interest are the glacial features of the crags and the wildlife. There should be no difficulty in route finding but there is a steep descent that can be slippery.

Cross the stile to the right of the stream and follow the path west into the **cwm** to a stone squeeze and a wooden gateway through the wall. Stop and read the information board after crossing the stile as it explains the purpose and code of conduct for the area. To the left of the stream is a laid out picnic area, with trestle tables and a good view of the cwm.

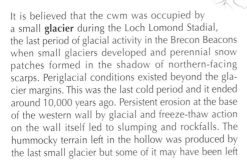

It is believed that the cwm was occupied by a small **glacier** during the Loch Lomond Stadial, the last period of glacial activity in the Brecon Beacons when small glaciers developed and perennial snow patches formed in the shadow of northern-facing scarps. Periglacial conditions existed beyond the glacier margins. This was the last cold period and it ended around 10,000 years ago. Persistent erosion at the base of the western wall by glacial and freeze-thaw action on the wall itself led to slumping and rockfalls. The hummocky terrain left in the hollow was produced by the last small glacier but some of it may have been left from the earlier Late Devensian ice-sheet that covered the entire Brecon Beacons around 20,000 years ago.

Take the waymarked route into the cwm. There are botanically interesting boggy areas which contain extraordinary species such as the carnivorous sundew (*Drosera rotundifolia*), which flowers between June and August. Ascend the steep slope, along a path in a north-westerly direction, crossing a number of stiles, to a small cairn. Cross another stile and continue diagonally left across a bilberry-covered slope to the top of **Craig Carrig-gleisiad**, where there is a stile in a fence that runs north–south. ◀

An ancient settlement site is marked on the map in the cwm.

Cross the fence and walk parallel to it (S) to a pool at SN960 221. A short distance further on there are two stiles near a T-junction of fences. There is a Countryside Council for Wales information board just before this spot.

Cross the stile on the right and continue along the path, keeping the fence on your left, following around the top of the crags. Take care when the path descends steeply east down a grassy slope. Cut north through a hole in the wall at SN971 220 and continue north, walking parallel to the fence. Cross the stream and join the path again on the opposite side. Retrace your steps (E) to the start.

View west of entrance to Craig Cerrig-gleisiad

CRAIG CERRIG-GLEISIAD À FAN FRYNYCH NATIONAL NATURE RESERVE

The mountainous area of Craig Cerrig-gleisiad and Fan Frynych is of special botanical and geomorphological interest. It is owned and managed as a National Nature Reserve by the Countryside Council for Wales.

Rare arctic-alpine plants are mainly found in the gullies of the steep crags, where a cold, damp 'micro-climate' exists and where they are protected from grazing animals. This special micro habitat allows them to exist at or near the southern limit of their range in Britain. Interesting species include purple saxifrage (*Saxifraga oppositifolia*), mossy saxifrage (*Saxifraga hypnoides*), green spleenwort (*Asplenium viride*), lesser meadow rue (*Thalictrum minus*) and northern bedstraw (*Galium boreale*). Moorland vegetation is made up largely of dwarf-shrub heathland comprising heather (*Calluna vulgaris*), bilberry (*Vaccinium myrtillus*), crowberry (*Empetrum nigrum*) and associated grasses such as wavy hair-grass (*Deschampsia flexuosa*) and mat-grass (*Nardus stricta*). Around 80 bird species can be found in the Reserve of which nearly 30 breed here. Skylark and meadow pipit are constant companions when walking over heathland, with buzzard, kestrel, peregrine falcon and raven often sighted wheeling overhead. Look out for ring ouzel around gullies, wheatear on boulder-strewn slopes, whinchat among bracken and heather, redstart and tree pipit in hawthorn scrub, and dipper and wagtail darting along streams.

The area is owned and managed primarily to benefit nature conservation by the Countryside Council for Wales. Objectives are to re-establish a diverse dwarf-shrub heathland dominated by heather and bilberry and to encourage development of scattered hawthorn on mid-slopes and a more dense cover of trees and shrubs on lower slopes. These will be achieved primarily by controlling the numbers of grazing stock and by selective tree planting.

For further information contact the Countryside Council of Wales – Unit 13B, Mill Street Industrial Estate, Mill Street, Abergavenny NP7 5HE Tel 01873 857938.

WALK 25
Fan Fawr

Start	Nant-yr-Eira Bridge (SN988 178)
Map required	Central Map OL11
Distance	9km (5.6 miles)
Total ascent	350m (947ft)

This unusual route to the summit of Fan Fawr avoids the busier direct approach from Storey Arms. The walk gains height gradually by following the crest of the glacial cwm. A circuit of the summit gives fine views in all directions, including the Carmarthen Fan to the west and the Tarell Valley to the north. The route is best saved for reasonably clear weather because route finding can be difficult in poor visibility. No great exertion is required and there are good views across to the highest of the Beacons and down into a glacial cwm and moraine.

From the bridge, climb up the left bank of the stream past a small waterfall and then above the stream bed where there are rowan trees. When the summit of Fan Fawr becomes visible the stream is crossed by some sandstone scars. Looking over to the north-east, the north-western ridge of Cefn Cwm Llwch rising up to Corn Du is visible, and the valley below it to the west contains the headwaters of the River Taff (Blaen Taff Fawr). South of this is the ridge above Cwm Crew. Note this as it will be a useful direction marker in later in this route.

Leave the stream at the sandstone outcrop and aim north for the southern ridge of Fan Fawr along **Cefn yr Henriw.** From here look down into the cwm below the summit where there is a **moraine**, Cefn Bach.

132

Looking back towards where you started is the most north-erly of the reservoirs – the Beacons reservoir.

*Fan Fawr from
Cefn yr Henriw*

The route follows the edge of the glacial cwm which gives Fan Fawr its character. A most interesting feature lies in its base. This is a linear moraine marked on the map as Cefn Bach which runs parallel to the ridge. This was probably formed when scree material from the back wall of the cwm slid down the surface of a snow bed which formed because it was sheltered from the sun's rays. This is called a **nivation ridge** or **protalus**. Another theory is that the moraine is of glacial origin and was formed when ice occupied the cwm.

Follow the ridge along a sheep track and this continues up to the **Fan Fawr** summit cairn, which is to the north-east of the trig point. To the east, the summit of Corn Du obscures Pen y Fan which at 886m (2907ft) is the highest point in South Wales. The ugly scar of the footpath leading from Pont ar Daf to Corn Du is all too evident on a clear day. Due west is a superb view of Bannau Sir Gaer, with the ridges of Fan Dringarth, Fan Nedd and Fan Gyhirych in the foreground.

133

On rounding the northern slope of Fan Fawr, the receding lines of the Fans are revealed in all their splendour. The western slopes of Fan Fawr fall away into Cwm Dringarth whose head holds the Ystradfellte reservoir.

Looking due north you see the buttress which hides Craig Cerrig-gleisiad, part of a National Nature Reserve (see Walk 24), in the valley behind.

Descend north from the summit cairn, following the top of the crags, until a steep slope is reached at SN973 196. At this point you meet the path which comes up the hill from Storey Arms. Follow the path which contours west around the north side of Fan Fawr or drop a little further down the slope and choose a contour just below the small rock outcrops. Look down onto the sheep folds or hafodydd below (see Walk 8). ◄

Eventually, you can follow a well-marked sheep track round to the south-west where it starts to climb a little. Contour round to the east side of Fan Fawr south of the trig point. Aim for the southern end of Cefn Crew ridge across the valley, keeping well above areas of bog marked by rushes on your left. Keep above the spring line on the hillside.

The walk back across the open moorland crosses many rivulets and these later coalesce to form the **Afon Hepste** which joins with the **Afon Mellte** in the spectacular waterfall valleys of Ystradfellte (see Section 5). This will bring you back

Raven

on the ridge (Cefn yr Henriw) you climbed earlier. Retrace your steps by descending this and then walking to the stream in a south-easterly direction to the scars at the stream bed. Cross here and descend the right bank back to the start.

WALK 26
Craig Cwm-du and Fan Frynych

Start	Near Forest Lodge Cottages (SN962 242)
Map required	Central Map OL11
Distance	7.5km (5 miles)
Total ascent	270m (886ft)

A medium-level walk with easy route finding in a relatively quiet part of the park. An easy approach along Sarn Helen, a Roman Road, brings you to the entrance to Craig Cwm-du – a place of outstanding beauty that may remind you of a miniature Scottish glen. The area is of exceptional nature conservation interest, being part of a National Nature Reserve (see Walk 24). An easy climb through slopes covered in heather and bilberry brings you to the top of Fan Frynych for fine views of the Brecon Beacons. There are no great difficulties in following the route, except on the climb to the summit of Fan Frynych. The area is quiet and unspoiled and presents a different character to other parts of the Beacons.

From the right-angle bend near **Forest Lodge Cottages**, take the stony track south-west to a gate just after which is a foot-path signed to Coed Ty Mawr. Ignore this and carry on a short distance, through a second gate. This straight track is **Sarn Helen**, a Roman Road. Continue to a third gate where a track leaves to the left. Make a mental note that this is your return route from the ridge up to your left where you can see a diagonal track leading down from the hill.

Pass through another gate and a few hundred metres beyond this on your right is a stile in the hill fence with a yellow arrow indicating a right of way down to Pontbren-garreg. Ignore this and continue to the next gate and cross the stile

135

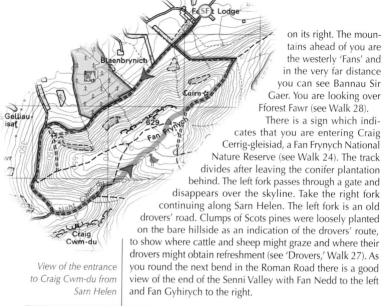

on its right. The mountains ahead of you are the westerly 'Fans' and in the very far distance you can see Bannau Sir Gaer. You are looking over Fforest Fawr (see Walk 28).

There is a sign which indicates that you are entering Craig Cerrig-gleisiad, a Fan Frynych National Nature Reserve (see Walk 24). The track divides after leaving the conifer plantation behind. The left fork passes through a gate and disappears over the skyline. Take the right fork continuing along Sarn Helen. The left fork is an old drovers' road. Clumps of Scots pines were loosely planted on the bare hillside as an indication of the drovers' route, to show where cattle and sheep might graze and where their drovers might obtain refreshment (see 'Drovers,' Walk 27). As you round the next bend in the Roman Road there is a good view of the end of the Senni Valley with Fan Nedd to the left and Fan Gyhirych to the right.

View of the entrance to Craig Cwm-du from Sarn Helen

136

SARN HELEN

This Roman road linked Neath and Brecon and eventually with the coast road running from Chester to Segontium. It is named after Helen, Welsh wife of the Romano-British emperor Magnus Maximus. She was St Helena, celebrated as the finder of the true cross and mother of the Emperor Constantine who was first declared emperor by the army in Britain. A 14th-century Welsh story in the 'Mabinogion' tells how Macsen Wledig – the Roman usurper Magnus Maximus – dreamt of a girl whom he later discovered in Arfon and married. As a wedding gift she asked for three strongholds to be built at Caernarfon, Caerleon and Carmarthen, to be joined by roads known as roads of 'Elen of the Hosts'. A 12th-century tradition, however, makes Helena the daughter of the founder of Colchester. The Romans had a hard struggle in controlling the Silures, a warlike Welsh tribe which ruled this mountainous part of South Wales prior to being conquered. In fact, from the time of the Roman invasion of Britain in AD43, it took them around 25 years to subdue the Silures. The Romans ruled Britain for nearly 300 years and finally left, their empire in ruins, in AD400. Sarn Helen continued to be an important road and was used by drovers taking their cattle and sheep to markets for many centuries.

Continue along Sarn Helen to where a track leaves to the left just before the bridge where there are ruins of an old toll house at the entrance to **Cwm-du**. The pool at the entrance to Cwm-du would have been used by drovers to water their cattle. Leave Sarn Helen by turning left up the track at the apex of the right-hand bend before the bridge.

Craig Cwm-du is part of a **National Nature Reserve** comprising 493 hectares of heathland and crags (see Walk 24). The southern valley side has been steepened by the action of ice, forming 150m-high crags on which grow a rich flora which includes arctic-alpine species.

Follow the track into the cwm to the fork in the stream. Take the left-hand branch. Towards the top, near the small waterfalls, is a sign indicating a left turn. Follow this, working up left slightly away from the stream to avoid impassable waterfalls in the stream bed. The stream forks again and you take the left branch up a small side valley on its left flank. Follow this to a bed of cotton-grass and reeds. Continue north-north-east arriving at **Fan Frynych** summit and meet the track from Craig Cerrig-gleisiad coming up from the right. Fan Frynych is a fine vantage point for views to the east of Corn Du and Pen y Fan.

From the trig point aim north-north-east, with the Brecon Beacons at about 2 o'clock, and pass close to small **quarry spoils**, leaving them on your right. This stony track drops down to the hill fence and gate. The impression is gained of descending into the Tarell Valley but on reaching the larch trees and two gates and a stile, turn sharp left and follow the clear track down to Sarn Helen. Turn right to return to the start of the walk.

WALK 27
Craig Cwm-du, Fan Dringarth and Fan Llia

Start	Sarn Helen (SN925 184)
Map required	Central Map OL11
Distance	16.25km (10.4 miles)
Total ascent	212m (696ft)

A walk full of interest, both past and present. The Romans constructed Sarn Helen road past Cwm-du, the Black Valley, which is now part of a National Nature Reserve. From the head of the cwm there are superb views of the rest of the reserve, the crags and gullies of Craig Cerrig-gleisiad. Both of these cwms have an astonishing variety of birdlife, including buzzards and peregrine falcons. The return route crosses over Fan Dringarth and Fan Llia before dropping into the Llia Valley. The walk is quite relaxed and not too difficult to follow and it is in a rarely visited area of the National Park. If you enjoy seclusion, this is a walk well worth considering.

At the point where Sarn Helen leaves the road, walk (NNE) up the stony track to the **ford** (Rhyd Uchaf). Sarn Helen is a Roman Road (see Walk 26). A few hundred metres further on, look left to see a large standing stone, **Maen Llia** (see Walk 28).

After 2.5km pass through a gate to a Countryside Council for Wales sign at the entrance to Cwm-du. Cwm-du has the feel of a Scottish glen and any moment one expects to see

DROVERS

There are many old tracks in the Brecon Beacons which were used for many centuries by drovers. These men transported livestock from the agricultural areas to markets in England. Cattle were shod to protect their feet on long journeys and geese had their feet dipped in tar. The drovers returned from the markets with various goods for the farmers. Interestingly, they brought back gorse seed which was sown on the friddland, the steep hillside, often enclosed, up to 300m. Young gorse shoots are, apparently, a delicacy to sheep but they also provided shelter for seedlings such as thorn. A hard winter may well kill off old gorse but the thorn seedlings may have grown just enough to survive grazing. A notable feature of the Brecon Beacons today are the dotted thorn trees on the valley sides, which provide good nesting sites for merlins.

a red deer moving among the Scots pines. It is the western half of a National Nature Reserve (see 'Craig Cerrig-gleisiad à Fan Frynych National Nature Reserve,' Walk 24). The pool at the entrance to Cwm-du would have been used by drovers to water their cattle.

Walking along Sarn Helen with Craig Cwm-du in the distance

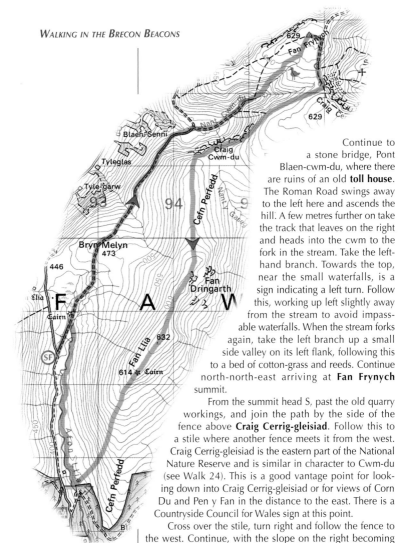

Continue to a stone bridge, Pont Blaen-cwm-du, where there are ruins of an old **toll house**. The Roman Road swings away to the left here and ascends the hill. A few metres further on take the track that leaves on the right and heads into the cwm to the fork in the stream. Take the left-hand branch. Towards the top, near the small waterfalls, is a sign indicating a left turn. Follow this, working up left slightly away from the stream to avoid impassable waterfalls. When the stream forks again, take the left branch up a small side valley on its left flank, following this to a bed of cotton-grass and reeds. Continue north-north-east arriving at **Fan Frynych** summit.

From the summit head S, past the old quarry workings, and join the path by the side of the fence above **Craig Cerrig-gleisiad**. Follow this to a stile where another fence meets it from the west. Craig Cerrig-gleisiad is the eastern part of the National Nature Reserve and is similar in character to Cwm-du (see Walk 24). This is a good vantage point for looking down into Craig Cerrig-gleisiad or for views of Corn Du and Pen y Fan in the distance to the east. There is a Countryside Council for Wales sign at this point.

Cross over the stile, turn right and follow the fence to the west. Continue, with the slope on the right becoming steeper all the time, until the high point of **Craig Cwm-du** is reached above the steepest crags. From this vantage point

above the crags are good views of Corn Du and Pen y Fan to the east and Fforest Fawr to the west (see Walk 28). The bowl-shaped hill is Fan Gyhirych and to its right and beyond is Bannau Sir Gaer. The summit on its left with the trig point is Fan Nedd.

Corn Du and Pen y Fan from Fan Dringarth

Leave the top of the crags and follow the track due south, arriving at a cairn just short of the summit of **Fan Dringarth**. Below on the left there is evidence of a quarry (see 'Geology of the Brecon Beacons,' Introduction). Look out for a variety of upland birds (see 'Birdlife,' Introduction).

Continue following the ridge (SSW) to the slightly higher summit of **Fan Llia**. A little further on are a number of peat pools and the site of an ancient **cairn**. Looking due south, the prominent ridge in the distance is the Rhigos. Beyond the ridge, and hidden by it, are the South Wales mining valleys. ▶

Fan Llia is covered by purple moor grass (*Molinia*) together with mat grass (*Nardus*) and heath rush (*Juncus squarrosus*). Soft rush (*Juncus effusus*) is common towards the southern end of the ridge.

The cairn provides a reference point to start the descent (SSW) to reach the stream of **Afon Llia** where the coniferous forestry fence drops down the hillside to the stream bed (SN926 166). Head upstream along the right-hand bank of the stream to Rhyd Uchaf. Pick up the Sarn Helen Roman Road here and turn sharp left to return to the start.

WALK 28
Fan Gyhirych and Fan Nedd

Start	South of Maen Llia (SN924 191)
Map required	Central Map OL11
Distance	10km (6.4 miles)
Total ascent	442m (1450ft)

These mountains are part of Fforest Fawr and are more rounded and gentle than the high peaks of the Brecon Beacons. The walk includes the summits of Fan Gyhirych and Fan Nedd and, although of reasonable length, is not too strenuous. Ascents and descents are gentle but there may be some difficulty in route finding in bad weather as the tracks are unfrequented. This area is recommended if you like solitude and there are some fine views to be enjoyed in clear weather.

Start about 100m south of the standing stone, **Maen Llia**, on the western side of the road where there is a stile. Soon after crossing the stile, turn right (NW) and follow a collapsed stone wall diagonally across the hillside up to the right to where a path leads along a wire fence.

Turn left (SW) along this path which cuts across the face of Fan Nedd. The valley lying before you is called Blaen Senni. This area is part of **Fforest Fawr**. As you turn the corner, the head of the valley becomes quite steep with a number of Brownstone crags leading down from the summit of

Senni valley

Fan Nedd on the left (see 'Geology of the Brecon Beacons,' Introduction). Before reaching the crags there is a fine panorama with sandstone blocks in the foreground, the head of the U-shaped valley in the middle-ground and Fan Gyhirych in the background (see 'Glacial origin of U-shaped valleys,' Introduction). Looking back to the north, there is a patchwork landscape of fields and natural woodland.

Climbing the valley the impressive cliff and cusp of Fan Gyhirych may be seen. Look back occasionally for views of the summits of Corn Du and Pen y Fan in the distance.

At SN911 191, cross the main gully which drains the slope above. This is attractive with heather and bilberry on both sides and a few rowan trees. The whole of the bed of the gully is carpeted with turf and moss and is dry in the summer but a frothy stream in winter.

The slope on the left eases and just before the col, join the permitted route which drops from the summit of Fan Nedd. Continue to the col between the valleys of Blaen Senni and the Nedd. From the col follow the fence on your right – this area can be boggy and very wet after a rainy period. At the end of the col is a fence and gate with a white arrow indicating a permitted footpath. Follow this sign up to the left.

FFOREST FAWR, THE GREAT FOREST OF BRECKNOCK

The broad upland area between Pen y Fan in the east and Carmarthen Fan in the west is known as Fforest Fawr, the Great Forest. The term 'forest' is a legal definition and denotes an area of land set aside for royalty for hunting. Fforest Fawr came under Forest Law after the Norman Conquests of the Welsh Princes in 1066. The formerly wooded valleys provided good cover for game and, in particular, red deer, a truly royal beast and an important source of fresh venison during the winter. The semi-fortified enclosure of Castell Coch at the confluence of Afon Dringarth and Afon Llia was in the heart of the Forest and may well have been the site of the Forest Court where offenders were tried. By the beginning of the 18th century the last deer had disappeared due to poaching and grazing competition with Commoners' flocks of sheep and herds of cattle. Fforest Fawr was split up by the 1815 Act of Enclosure, and of the original 39,390 acres, 21,484 acres were withdrawn from the Common and sold to private landholders. The funds raised by the Crown were supposedly to finance wars but in fact they were used for the building of Regent Street in London.

From this point, looking back down the Blaen Senni Valley, there are fine views into Cwm-du (see Walk 26), the western half of Craig Cerrig-gleisiad à Fan Frynych National Nature Reserve (see Walk 24). The line at the top of the green fields is, more or less, where Sarn Helen, the Roman Road, runs and to the right of this the two highest peaks of the Brecon Beacons are clearly in view, Corn Du (Black Horn) to the right and Pen y Fan to the left.

About 15m past the gatepost, cross a derelict stone wall. Cut across the field, climbing diagonally up the slope to a wire fence. Follow this to the apex of fences. The Rhigos Mountain forms the skyline to the left. Nearing the apex of this field, climb over the brow of the hill and directly ahead is a gate in the fence leading to an obvious track. This gate is signposted with a white permitted footpath arrow. ◄

Beyond is the impressive sweeping cliff of Fan Gyhirych on the extreme western edge of the Central Brecon Beacons map.

Go straight across the track as the route is made more interesting by skirting around the cwm above the headwall. Coming over the brow of the hill can be seen the fine profile of Bannau Sir Gaer, the Carmarthen Fan. Below to the right is the Cray reservoir and in the foreground is a private forestry plantation. Looking back from this point, there is a good view of the Brecon Beacons. The upper third part of the back slope of the cwm in front of Fan Gyhirych is marked by a resistant rock band which marks an abrupt change of slope.

Overgrazing by sheep has resulted in a loss of heather moorland. This is replaced by bent and fescue grassland, often intermixed with mat grass. Britain's only deciduous grass, purple moor grass, grows in wetter areas such as the moor between Penderyn and the Mellte. Its dead leaves can be found trapped on wire fences after winter storms. Tragically, the Forestry Commission has attempted to drain and plant conifers here, causing considerable damage to the peat bog habitat.

As you follow the edge of the cwm, the ground to the right becomes much steeper. The surface on this side of the headwall of Fan Gyhirych has a crenulated appearance from the myriad sheep tracks that have crossed it horizontally. This imparts a kind of ripple effect as it is combined with soil creep. Some of the uppermost ledges are partly inaccessible to grazing sheep and have an interesting flora. Green spleenwort (*Asplenium viride*), brittle bladder-fern (*Cystopteris fragilis*), northern bedstraw (*Galium boreale*), *Phegopteris*

Head of the Senni Valley and Fan Gyhirych

connectilis and cliff meadow rue (*Thalictrum minus*) are found here, together with a collection of uncommon bryophytes found only in rocky upland areas.

From the rounded summit of **Fan Gyhirych** look down south-west to the Neath Valley with Pontneddfechan in the middle ground and the Rhigos massif in the background. On the far horizon, looking south of Fan Gyhirych, is the conspicuous smoke stack at Baglan Bay. The stretch of water to the right of this is Mumbles Bay. To the east is Fan Nedd which has a steep slope to the left. Beyond, in the distance, are the Black Mountains to the left of Pen y Fan. Further to the left of Pen y Fan, you may see the town of Brecon.

From the top of the headwall, cross west to the trig point about 400m away. Once at the trig point, look west for a good view of Fan Hir which leads up to Bannau Sir Gaer. The summit is covered by peat on which grows hare's tail grass (*Eriophorum vaginatum*) mire. Common cotton-grass (*E. angustifolium*) can be found, together with wavy hair grass (*Deschampsia flexuosa*) and heath rush (*Juncus squarrosus*).

Continue west of the trig point for a view over the Swansea Valley. Down to the left are the spectacular limestone caves of Dan-yr-Ogof and the high land above is their catchment area. ◄ Fan Gyhirych is one of the finest panoramic viewpoints in South Wales.

Retrace your steps to the trig point at the summit and follow the permitted right of way down to the gate where you meet the obvious track again. Retrace your outward route by turning right through a gate indicated by a white path arrow. Head downslope in the direction of **Fan Nedd**, returning to the col and take the path which winds up the ridge to the trig point on the summit.

On the last few stretches of the climb, you come across a number of eroded peat haggs (see Walk 20). Loss of peat here has been slowed down considerably by recolonising plants. Finally, the slope eases and you end up walking over Nardus grassland gently to the summit. Vegetation here is a mixture of hare's tail grass (*Eriophorum vaginatum*), mat grass (*Nardus*) and bilberry (*Vaccinium myrtillus*), with frequent common cotton-grass (*E. angustifolium*), wavy hair grass (*Deschampsia flexuosa*) and some crowberry (*Empetrum nigrum*) growing on peat up to a metre deep.

Below the caves can be seen, with the aid of binoculars, the house of Madam Adelina Patti, the famous opera soprano.

From the summit of Fan Nedd take a bearing north-east and follow the track down to the road past the earthwork marked on the map. You meet the road opposite the standing stone of Maen Llia. ▸ The standing stone is very impressive and well worth a visit.

> Maen Llia is a Bronze Age standing stone that has served as a distinctive waymark for thousands of years. Erected by the Beaker folk about 4000 years ago, it is at least 4m high, 3m across and almost 1m thick and has a mystical aura about it due, in part, to the mythical story that this huge stone disappears at cockcrow when it is said to go down to the river.

Bog cotton

The north-east slope of Fan Nedd is carpeted in a springy cover of ling (*Calluna vulgaris*) in places.

147

5 WATERFALL COUNTRY

Sgwd Gwladus frozen during the winter of 2009

WALK 29
Pontneddfechan Waterfalls

Start	Old White Horse Inn, Pontneddfechan (SN902 077)
Map required	Central Map OL11
Distance	8km (5 miles)
Total ascent	Negligible

This is a low-level walk around the beautiful riverside scenery of the Afon Pyrddin and the Afon Nedd. The route is easily followed and includes a number of impressive waterfalls. Autumn is the best season for a visit as the route is entirely through deciduous forestry. Paths are well marked and no great effort is required to complete the route, even in bad weather. The river geology is very interesting and there is evidence of old industrial and mining activity in the valley. After heavy rain the rivers are in spate and the waterfalls are at their best. The walk returns to the Old White Horse Inn where you will find a warm welcome, good food and real ale.

From the Old White Horse Inn (Tafarn yr Hen Geffyl Gwyn) walk to the bridge across the Afon Nedd. A wrought iron sign indicates that the path leads to the White Lady Falls (Sgwd Gwladus). Pass through the cast-iron kissing gates and follow the wide track up the left (W) side of the river.

There are good exposures of the rock strata beside the path in a large sandstone cliff on the left. This is the Farewell Rock, so called as it marked the end of the Coal Measures. Numerous plant fossil fragments can be seen if you look up at the undersurface of the bedding planes, indicating that these rocks were formed on land some 316 million years ago when Wales was in the tropics. The dip of the Millstone Grit beds to the south is clearly evident, especially in the strata exposed in the river gorge. Take some time to read an interpretation panel on the right shortly after you start the walk.

This track was once an old tramway and you can still see the stone sleepers in place with holes in them for fixing the rails. It was used for transporting silica rock from mines further up the valley.

149

THE TRAVELS OF GIRALDUS CAMBRENSIS

Giraldus Cambrensis, the son of a Norman Baron and a Welsh Princess, wrote *Itinerarium Cambriae*, or *Journey of Wales*, in the late 12th century. He travelled around Wales, spreading propaganda supporting the Crusades, and recorded many interesting stories. One of these concerned Elidyr, who lived in the upper Neath Valley in the fourth century. Elidyr was learning to read at the age of 12 but was frequently beaten by his disciplinarian teacher and, to escape his wrath, ran away and hid in a hollow along the banks of the Afon Nedd.

After two days he was hungry and miserable but then two tiny men appeared who offered to take him to a land where all was play-time and pleasure. They led him through a dark underground tunnel to a beautiful country but it was rather dark as the sun did not shine here. The people of this world never lied and lived on a vegetarian diet. Elidyr became friends with the King's son but frequently returned to the upper world where he told only his mother of his adventures. His mother asked him to bring her back a present of gold, a common metal in the land. Elidyr returned with a golden ball which he stole while playing with the King's son. The little people caught up with him as he tripped on the doorstep of his house, snatching the ball and running off with it making remarks of scorn and derision to Elidyr. Realising his foolish act, Elidyr ran back to the river but the entrance to the underground tunnel had gone.

The track continues through hazel and sycamore past a number of old mill workings (one on the left with five granite mill stones) and drops back down to the river. The path is wide and good enough here for wheelchairs. It goes through a gate or stile where on the left is an old flooded mine working with three adits branching from the entrance.

On a hot summer's day the air in the tunnels is surprisingly cool but in the winter it feels warm and muggy. The reason for this is that the air in underground passages remains at a constant temperature of 4°C regardless of the season. Beyond, on the left, is a bricked entrance to another working and there are others on the far side of the river where a small side valley, Cwm Gored, branches off from here.

After a picnic area the path narrows and climbs slightly up some wooden steps, clearly now not suitable for wheelchairs. After a short distance the confluence of the rivers is reached at a deep pool just below a footbridge.

INDUSTRY ALONG THE NEDD FECHAN

The flooded adits that lead underground on the west side of the Nedd Fechan were once worked for silica, almost 100% SiO_2, by about thirty miners. These are just part of a more extensive system of mine workings on both sides of the river. The abutments of three bridges, which once took tramways to the eastern bank, can be seen by the observant walker on the opposite side of the river, with one in particular being in good condition on the far side but totally absent from the western bank. Silica mining in the valley began in the 1822 and carried on for nearly a hundred years.

William Weston Young discovered how to make firebricks from Dinas Silica which were used all over Europe and America to line iron and steel making furnaces, limekilns and domestic fire places. The rock was crushed in the valley and then transported by horse-drawn tram to the firebrick factory at Pont Walby, which closed in 1920.

The hard sandstone was also used for making millstones. The remains of a double-race mill are passed on the left bank. This was used to grind corn grown by local farmers. Dinas rock was quarried for limestone, which was transported to Pont Walby where it was crushed and either heated to produce lime for agricultural use or used for road metalling.

Horseshoe Falls

Do not cross the footbridge if water levels are low but continue north-west on the left bank of the **Afon Pyrddin** to a viewing platform before Sgwd Gwladus. Scramble down to the stream bed, pass carefully behind the fall and use the boulders as stepping stones to gain the bank on the other side. These stones are submerged if the river is in spate and you will have to return to the bridge, cross it, and visit **Sgwd Gwladus** via the northern bank. After passing behind the fall, up above on the damp rock is an interesting collection of wet-loving plants such as ferns.

SGWD GWLADUS

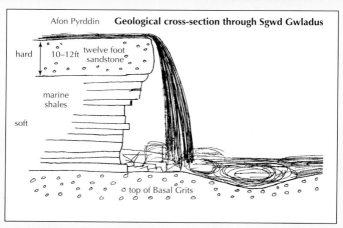

Afon Pyrddin   **Geological cross-section through Sgwd Gwladus**

hard   10–12ft twelve foot sandstone

marine shales

soft

top of Basal Grits

Sgwd is Welsh for waterfall and comes from the verb *ysgwd*, which means to toss or fling. This fall has been popular with tourists for many years and is known by English visitors as Lady Fall. The Welsh name comes from Gwladys, a daughter of the fifth-century King Brychan of Brycheiniog who had 24 daughters and 12 sons! Brychan was, unusually for his time, of Goidelic or Irish descent.

Sgwd Gwladus occurs where the Afon Pryddin encounters a resistant band of Millstone Grit sandstone. The middle part of the geological formation known as the Millstone Grit consists mostly of black, crumbling shales but there are layers of hard sandstone, the most important of which is the 'twelve foot sandstone' which occurs 13m above the base of the shale division. The general level of the Pyrddin is above the surface of this massive band of grit. Upstream of Sgwd Gwladus, the Pyrddin rapidly cut a steep gorge through the weak upper shales, the floor of the gorge being, for some distance, the surface of the twelve foot sandstone itself. The black shales exposed in the face of the fall are easily eroded by water and, from time to time, blocks of the overhanging massive sandstone bed become undermined so much that they collapse. The waterfall is slowly migrating upstream as a result, as well as laterally to the west due to the inclination of the strata in this direction.

In dry conditions, the water comes over the extreme left side of the bedding plane which forms the top of the fall. When the river is in spate, the fall comes down in a single sheet which extends across to the right.

Climb up above the fall to the **rocking stone**, a large boulder in the river bed, which has unfortunately been vandalised and is now immobile. The right bank can be explored for only a short distance upstream before it becomes impassable without wading the river. From here follow the eastern bank downstream back to the bridge. This is a popular place in warm weather with swimmers dropping into the pool below from a rope swing.

Back at the bridge do not cross it but follow the left bank of the left-hand tributary, the **Nedd Fechan**. ▶

This path takes you high above the gorge which has a number of small waterfalls (see 'Rivers of the Waterfall Country,' Walk 30). In a short distance, the path falls to the level of the river where there are a number of rapids. On the left side, near these falls, is a lovely small stream cascading over moss-covered rocks. As you follow the bend from the rapids, deep river pools can be seen and above these are the photogenic and aptly named Horseshoe Falls. Above these are the Lower and Upper Sgwd Ddwli.

Approach the Lower Sgwd Ddwli either via the flat rocks in the river bed (if the water is low) or by a track up to the left if they are covered. The Lower Sgwd Ddwli falls are in two sections, the second part being higher than the first and in an enclosed cliff area. To continue upstream from Lower Sgwd Ddwli retrace your steps along the stream bed. Walk about 20m to the end of the crags (above to the right) and scramble up the slope to gain the path above. About 50m above Lower Sgwd Ddwli is a pool about 6m in depth, which

A short detour (400m) can be made across the bridge to Cwm Gored to visit the entrance to the largest silica mine in the valley.

153

was once cut by the Upper Sgwd Ddwli waterfall. This fall is some 200m further upstream around a bend in the river. If you are lucky, a dipper may pose in the foreground (see 'Birdlife,' Introduction).

Retrace your steps to the footbridge and back down the western bank of the Afon Nedd to Pontneddfechan.

WALK 30
Waterfall Walk

Start	Pontneddfechan (SN902 077)
Map required	Central Map OL11
Distance	18km (11.2 miles)
Total ascent	Negligible

This is a low-level walk around the beautiful riverside scenery of the Afon Pyrddin, Afon Nedd, Afon Mellte and Afon Hepste. The route is well defined and includes a number of impressive waterfalls. Autumn is the best season for a visit as the route is mostly through deciduous forestry but during exceptionally hard winters the waterfalls freeze, providing some spectacular scenes. Although not strenuous in terms of ascents or descents, the distance covered is considerable and the ground may be rough and slippery so that progress is slow. This is a highly recommended route with some of the finest river scenery in South Wales.

From the Old White Horse Inn (Tafarn yr Hen Geffyl Gwyn) walk to the bridge across the Afon Nedd. Pass through the cast-iron kissing gates and follow the wide track up the left (W) side of the river. The track continues through hazel and sycamore past a number of old mill and drops back down to the river. After a picnic area the path narrows and climbs slightly up some wooden steps. A short distance later the confluence of the rivers is reached at a deep pool just below a footbridge.

Do not cross the footbridge if water levels are low but continue north-west on the left bank of the **Afon Pyrddin** to a viewing platform before Sgwd Gwladus. Scramble down to the

stream
bed, pass
carefully behind the fall and use
the boulders as stepping stones to gain the bank on the other
side. These stones are submerged if the river is in spate and
you will have to return to the bridge, cross it, and visit Sgwd
Gwladus via the northern bank.

Climb up above the fall to the rocking stone, a large
boulder in the river bed, which has unfortunately been vandalised and is now immobile. From here follow the eastern
bank downstream back to the bridge.

Back at the bridge do not cross it but follow the left bank
of the left-hand tributary, the Nedd Fechan. As you follow
the bend from the rapids, deep river pools can be seen and
above these are the photogenic and aptly named Horseshoe
Falls. Above these are the Lower and Upper Sgwd Ddwli.

Approach the Lower Sgwd Ddwli either via the flat rocks
in the river bed (if the water is low) or by a track up to the left
if they are covered. To continue upstream from Lower Sgwd
Ddwli retrace your steps along the stream bed. Walk about

20m to the end of the crags (above to the right) and scramble up the slope to gain the path above. About 50m above Lower Sgwd Ddwli is a pool about 6m in depth which was once cut by the Upper Sgwd Ddwli waterfall. This fall is some 200m further upstream around a bend in the river.

After the falls, the gorge is left behind. Follow a grassy path along the western bank of the river. After a short distance, cross a stile leading to a picnic area. Cross the grassed picnic area to the car park and onto the road. Turn right across **Pont Melin-fach** and follow the road up the hill, ignoring the first stile on the left just over the bridge. Take the next stile on the left and cross the fields, coming back to the road again. A permitted footpath leaves the road just past the turning to Glynmercher-uchaf. Follow this along the stream and through the woodland to **Heol Fawr Farm** and on to a tarmac lane.

Where the lane turns sharp left there is a finger post to Capel Hermen. Turn right along a muddy farm track to a stile on the left and a second stile. Cross this and aim straight across the field to a stile opposite a church. Turn right down the road, passing a small shop on the right and a garage with a telephone box on the left. Continue down the road, crossing a cattle grid and just after this on the left is a limestone chipping car park. Take the track on the left to a gate and information board to the Waterfall Country.

After about 60m follow the finger post which directs you right at a fork in the track. Pass **Clyn-gwyn Farm** on your left and go through a gate before entering deciduous woodland. Soon you will hear the roar of the **Afon Mellte** as it plunges over the waterfall of **Sgwd Clun-gwyn**. Drop through the woods to a junction of paths with the waterfall straight ahead. Ignore the turning back to the right and continue left along the western bank to the top of the waterfall. Descend the steep slope to the top of the fall. The deep pools above the fall are ideal for a refreshing dip on warm summer days.

From the top of Sgwd Clun-gwyn, the adventurous can leap across the river just above the fall where the water runs in a narrow channel. If the river is in spate, walk upstream a few hundred metres to a bridge. Cross this, turn right and follow the east bank through woodland keeping as close to the river bed as possible. A narrow path with steep drops on the right skirts beneath an outcrop of Millstone Grit to a good vantage point above the fall. Continue along the distinct path to the next falls.

SGWD CLUN-GWYN (WHITE MEADOW FALL)

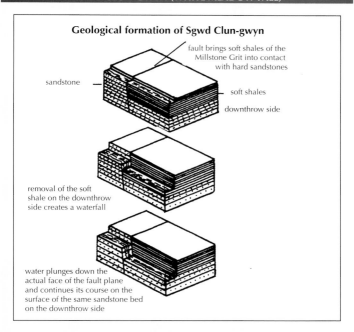

Geological formation of Sgwd Clun-gwyn

fault brings soft shales of the Millstone Grit into contact with hard sandstones

sandstone

soft shales

downthrow side

removal of the soft shale on the downthrow side creates a waterfall

water plunges down the actual face of the fault plane and continues its course on the surface of the same sandstone bed on the downthrow side

Sgwd Clun-gwyn is found on the Afon Mellte where it tumbles over a resistant massive band of Millstone Grit sandstone. The lower parts of the fall can be explored by scrambling down its side, using tree roots and good rock handholds, to a middle terrace and then down to the stream bed. When only a little water is flowing, it is possible to walk along the middle terrace for a closer look at the mosses and ferns which thrive in this very damp environment. A deep trough has been carved at the bottom of the fall by the tremendous scouring power of the falling water.

The fall was formed by earth movements bringing shales of the middle Millstone Grit into contact with the pebbly grit that constitutes the lowest stratigraphical member of the same formation. The weak shales are downstream of this geological fault which now forms the near-vertical face of the waterfall. This same fault crosses the Hepste around 1km to the south-south-east but ▶

157

the amount of earth movement dies out in this direction and an obvious feature has not formed in the Hepste. The shales were rapidly eroded by tumbling water and have, in fact, been removed completely downstream of the fall, as the river now runs across the same sandstone surface below the fall as it does above. This massive band of sandstone, known as the 'twelve foot sandstone', is the same as the overhanging bed over which Sgwd Gwladus plunges (see Walk 29). The fall has been working its way to the east as the tilt of the sandstone bedding forces the water in this direction.

A cross-section of the fault can be found clearly exposed on the eastern bank in line with the top of the waterfall. A good view of this can be found from the opposite bank immediately above the lip of the fall but foliage may obscure this. Looking along the line of the fall, you will see a deep narrow gully in the opposite bank. The weak shales on the right of the fault, the downthrown side, have suffered considerable disruption, whereas the competent massive sandstone bed on the left, the upthrown side, has suffered little internal fracturing. Shattering of the shales for some distance adjacent to the fault has further reduced their ability to withstand erosion. The fact that the fault plane which forms the face of the waterfall is still in line with the trace of the fault in the bank means that Sgwd Clun-gwyn has, unusually, not migrated upstream since its inception, in stark contrast with Sgwd yr Eira (see Walk 31).

Lower Sgwd Ddwli

At the top of **Sgwd Isaf Clun-gwyn**, climb down in front of the cliff where it is possible to walk along the edge to look at the upper cascade. Scramble around by the side of the pools and the falls. Descend to the lower pool of this sequence of falls and follow the bank of the river downstream.

SGWD ISAF CLUN-GWYN

This complex of cascades was formed by two parallel faults, fractures in the earth's crust, which brought a long narrow band of pebbly sandstones to the surface. The Mellte generally flows north–south along the outcrop of the middle shales of the Millstone Grit but the band of pebbly sandstone deflects its course to the west, crossing the sandstone by the shortest route and then turning south again once on a narrow tract of shale between the Farewell Rock (the Upper Millstone Grit sandstone) to the west and pebbly sandstone to the east. This present course is anomalous, as the river would not change direction to the west in order to cross a resistant band of rock when by continuing due south it would stay on weaker shales. The likely explanation for this strange course is that it was predetermined by a fault in the shale which overlay the faulted wedge of grit. This shale was then removed by erosion but the stream continued to flow in the same direction, a phenomenon known as 'superimposed' drainage.

Below the falls, there is a wide picnic area and the ground on the east of the river is quite flat. On the right-hand side is a very steep cliff. Proceed down the river to another small fall, **Sgwd y Pannwr** (Fall of the Fuller).

Continue down the valley by leaving the fall via a path which drops down the slope from the left and crosses Millstone Grit boulders. Shortly turn right, crossing more boulders, along a distinct path which climbs diagonally up the slope. The path narrows and runs three-quarters of the way up the side of the gorge – care is needed here, as there are precipitous drops to the stream bed far below. From this path there are wonderful views looking down to where the river bed becomes quite wide in places. The path is steep and hard and the public right of way along the top of the gorge is easier to follow.

Once round the bend in the river, follow the path which drops to the river bed. An easier route climbs to the top of the gorge and follows it to the junction of a number of paths. Continue straight on and follow the path which swings around to the left and into the Hepste Valley. This drops through woodland to the base of a Millstone Grit cliff (see 'Geological Rock Formations of the Waterfall Country,' Walk 33). Below is the end of a series of cascades. Down to the right, there are some small falls and the gorge becomes much narrower again. The path descends to river level and continues along the eastern bank to the confluence of the Afon Mellte and the **Afon Hepste** joining from the left.

Once at the confluence of the rivers, climb the steep prow ahead, as the Hepste gorge which swings around to the left is impassable at river level. This slippery climb can be avoided by staying on the top of the gorge instead of dropping to the stream bed. A path leads across about halfway up the slope. This joins the main path which zigzags its way down from the top. Follow this and drop down to the river bed again. ◀

The path descends to the river on a grassy bank then cuts up left via the river bed. Beyond this grassy bank, there is a series of falls in a narrow gorge, the **Lower Cilhepste Falls** (see Walk 32). Pass these by climbing up to the left and continue upstream. It is quite a steep climb up the rock to get to the left of these falls above the main ones. Keep close to the river past the last three cascades. Turn the corner and in front is the waterfall, **Sgwd yr Eira**. The path scrambles up over the stones on the left bank (looking upstream) and then passes behind the cascade. If there is a lot of water flowing, the wall on the left is quite wet and waterproofs are recommended (see 'Sgwd yr Eira,' Walk 31).

After passing behind Sgwd yr Eira, the path leads up the steep slope to the left. Part of this climb is a bouldery stream bed but towards the top there is a man-made zigzag of wooden ledges and posts. Don't deviate to the left but take the steps to the right, following a small valley in the side of

During March, April and May the striking white blossom of the blackthorn is very noticeable when you are walking through the woodland.

Blackthorn

the main gorge. The path doubles back on itself, arriving at the edge of some coniferous forestry where there are large stone boulders. The track to the left goes towards Penderyn but take the path to the right along the top of the gorge.

The path which ascends the steep gully has a **geological fault** running through it which was responsible for the original formation of the waterfall, which has since retreated upstream. The boulders at the top of the gully are glacial erratics and were transported by ice from another area and then left behind when the ice melted and the glacier retreated.

Walking along this well-cleared path, look down into the beautifully wooded gorge and the confluence of the two rivers. This piece of rather interesting land, which is owned by the Forestry Commission, is marked by a post sunk into the ground with a white band around it.

ANCIENT WOODLAND

Woodland clinging to the gorge walls of the Afon Mellte, Hepste, Sychryd, Nedd and Pyrddin forms one of the richest and most extensive areas of ancient semi-natural woodland in Wales. A wide variety of botanical types have been identi-fied, 10 in all, ranging from ash-maple woods on limestone to sessile oak-downy birch-wood sorrel types on Millstone Grit (see 'Geological rock formations of the Waterfall Country,' Walk 33). Downy birch-purple moor grass and alder-ash woods are found on wet ground conditions. Wet flushes in this type of woodland provide a home for marsh hawk's-beard (*Crepis paludosa*), its most southerly locality in Britain.

The sheer steepness and inaccessibility of the gorge walls have prevented timber exploitation in the past, leaving an ancient woodland almost untouched by Man in places. Only small pockets of truly ancient woodland survive today in Britain. Small-leaved lime thrives on cliff edges and steep slopes and is found together with wood fescue grass (*Festuca altissima*). The undisturbed nature of the woodland means that it still has its rich complement of woodland associ-ated species. This includes a number of rare ferns such as Wilson's filmy fern (*Hymenophyllum wilsonii*), Tunbridge filmy fern (*H. tunbrigense*), hay scented fern (*Dryopteris aemula*) and rare liverworts, mosses and lichens. These are found in a variety of habitats such as boulder scree, cliff faces, springs, decaying wood, ancient trees and numerous niches associated with streams and rivers.

The path leaves the top of the gorge and heads south. The hill ahead in the distance is the Rhigos Mountain, with a number of glacial corries in it. Beyond it is the South Wales coalfield and the valley to the south-west is the Neath.

The route swings right and down towards the gorge around the ruins of **Cilhepste-fach**. At this point leave the waymarked footpath, following the ride which runs west through the coniferous forestry. Beyond the forestry, pick up the line of a collapsed stone wall and look out for a conspicuous oak tree near the edge of the gorge at the end of a spur of land. This marks the beginning of the steep descent of an ill-defined zigzag path to an easy path along the eastern bank of the river below. Turn left on reaching this path.

Follow this distinct path downstream to the last waterfall on the Hepste, which is in two tiers. Continue downstream past a small brick structure and on to the weir. The extensive collection of ruined buildings, weirs and leats in the lower reaches of the valley were once a **gunpowder works** (see Walk 32).

From the weir, a well-made path continues along the side of the river, which is now quite wide. The path arrives at a flat area with some pleasant old woodland. Beyond the flat boggy area, where alder grows, is a constriction in the river. In the middle of the river bed is a block of rock which

Upper Sgwd Ddwli

RIVERS OF THE WATERFALL COUNTRY

The rivers of the Waterfall Country, the Mellte, Hepste, Sychryd, Pyrddin and the upper parts of the Neath, flowed into the Cynon Valley to the south-west. Earth movements during late Tertiary times uplifted this area, accelerating the rate at which South Wales' rivers were cutting valleys. The River Neath was particularly 'rejuvenated' and greatly extended its course north-east, utilising a line of weakness along a narrow belt of greatly folded and faulted rocks, the Neath Disturbance. The River Neath managed to capture the rivers of the Waterfall Country so that they flowed faster into the lower levels of the Neath. The rejuvenated rivers cut steep-sided gorges as waterfalls receded upstream.

is tilted at about 45° towards the west. Cross over the top of this and jump across to the stone structure. Scramble up the side of these broken-down blocks or make a detour to the left to get back to the path. To avoid the jump across the blocks, return back up the river until it is possible to climb up to your right to a path which eventually drops down to the wooden bridge.

Do not cross the wooden bridge but head straight across the grassy meander ahead to gain a distinct path along the side of the river. Continue past a stilling station on the far bank. Follow the track down to the bridge and the impressive cliff of **Craig y Ddinas**. An old tram route ran past Craig y Ddinas connecting the silica mine with the Vale of Neath Canal (see 'Industry along the Nedd Fechan,' Walk 29).

The extended walk to the Sychryd Valley leaves from here. To continue on the main route follow the road out of the car park across the river and walk back to the start in Pontneddfechan.

Extension

From Craig y Ddinas, there is an option of visiting the Sychryd Valley with its waterfalls and silica mines. Go into the car park and follow the footpath leading to the right of the crags. Walk into the narrow gorge with the stream below on the right. Rounding the corner, pass below an impressive cliff. Further up, this gorge becomes very narrow and the river tumbles down over a series of rocks at Sgydau Sychryd. The spectacular rock exposure at the entrance to the gorge on the right is called Bwa Maen. This impressive fold can only be clearly seen during winter months when it is not obscured by foliage.

Bwa Maen means 'bow rock' and well describes the spectacularly exposed arch-like fold with a sharp crest. If you look closely at the large boulders that have fallen from the roof of a cave, you will see that the rounded convex surfaces have small grooves. These are formed by the beds of rock rubbing together when they were being folded. The Carboniferous limestone was squeezed into this contorted feature by Amorican earth movements associated with the Neath Disturbance. A fault occurs immediately to the left of Bwa Maen, along which the Sychryd now flows.

Retrace your steps back to Craig y Ddinas and continue on the main route back to the start of the walk.

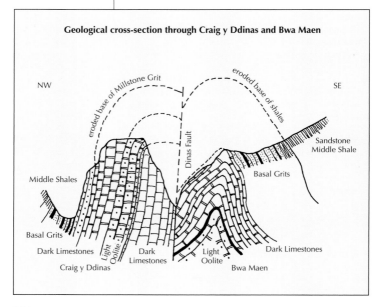

Geological cross-section through Craig y Ddinas and Bwa Maen

WALK 31
Sgwd yr Eira

Start	Penderyn (SN945 089)
Map required	Central Map OL11
Distance	10km (6 miles)
Total ascent	Negligible

This is an excellent walk, packed full of interest, culminating in an unforgettable experience of walking behind a waterfall. An initial easy ascent of Moel Penderyn is followed by an exploration of the Sychryd and Hepste Valleys where you will see evidence of a busy industrial past. Old ruins are left behind as you wind your way through the picturesque Hepste gorge with its tumbling river and steep slopes covered in ancient woodland. The best is left to last when you climb out of the Hepste Valley and drop into the Mellte gorge and walk behind Sgwd yr Eira, the Fall of Snow. The paths are reasonably easy to follow and there are good views in the early part of the walk followed by spectacular river scenery. The Red Lion, a few hundred metres south of the end of this walk, is full of character with fine ales and open fires.

From Penderyn take the track (W) towards the old quarries, through a gate with the distinctive yellow National Park arrow marking the route. Continue straight ahead to another gate and cross the stile. Turn immediately left following the hill

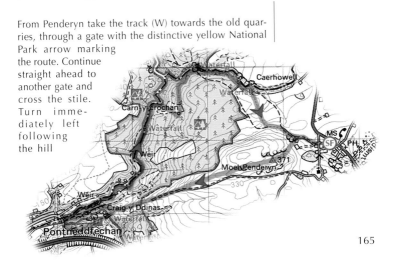

fence, leaving some quarry spoils on your right. Work up to the col ahead and then leave the fence and cross west to the summit of **Moel Penderyn** marked by a trig point.

North and slightly west from here you can see Fan Nedd with the Carmarthen Fans further to the west. North-east lie the Brecon Beacons. To the west of the road is the line of the Afon Hepste and to the east are the hills of Cefn Cadlan.

There are many clues on the map as to the rock type of this area such as numerous 'Areas of Shake Holes' and 'Swallow Holes'. These are typical of **limestone country** and, in fact, this area is a honeycomb of underground passages. The limestone is mostly capped by a layer of Millstone Grit. Swallow holes literally 'swallow' streams when they disappear underground, whereas shake holes are formed when the roof of an underground chamber or passage caves in. The Millstone Grit has often collapsed when the limestone beneath has been dissolved away. The Afon Hepste has changed its underground course many times, moving further south and west, leaving behind an extensive system of caves with spectacular stalagmites and stalactites. Limestone is mainly composed of calcium carbonate, which is slightly soluble in water. Limestone is more vigorously dissolved if weak acids are present in the water. In fact, groundwater which formed remarkable cave systems in South Wales is slightly acidic – a result of acid rain and from humic acids produced in soil and the breakdown of coniferous pine needles.

To the east is the massive limestone quarry (Cwar Llwyn-on) overlooking the village. To the south-east is the Cynon Valley and over to the south-west is the Rhigos Mountain with open cast coal mines on its flanks. Beyond and due west is the Swansea Valley.

Walk due west along the crest of the ridge. A close look at the rock outcrops here reveals that the limestone pavement has been polished by water, indicating that this area once suffered the powerful scouring action of a stream. **Moel Penderyn** is also geologically interesting for a different reason. Compressive forces in the earth's crust have pushed the rock strata into the form of an elongated dome, technically known as a pericline. The axis of this fold, known as the Penderyn Anticline, runs for many kilometres north-eastwards into the Old Red Sandstone and south-westwards into the Coal Measures (see 'Geology of the Brecon Beacons,' Introduction). This fold was formed during the Caledonian mountain building period as a result of north-westward compression. Beyond the ridge is a bilberry and cotton-grass heath.

Drop left before you reach a forestry fence to a track, known as the Ridgeway, which connected Penderyn with Pontneddfechan. The Ridgeway is an old drovers' road (see Walk 27). Follow this through a gate, heading in the direction of the head of the Neath Valley, dropping over the brow of the hill. Pass the ruins of **Clwyd-rhyd-fan** to reach mixed woodland. The track winds between spoil-heaps from old silica mines to a wooden sign with a marker pointing back to Penderyn. Looking back you can see the entrance to some of the mines. At this point you can either take the

Afon Mellte near the gunpowder works

rising track ahead to **Craig y Ddinas** or, for the alternative route, take the path off to the left signposted to the silica mines.

From Craig y Ddinas take the path north-east, signposted to the gunpowder works. This travels along the eastern bank of the **Afon Mellte** through woodland to a small open area where an obvious path goes up to the right. Ignore this and follow the river bank to a wooden bridge.

A sign points to the gunpowder works over the bridge and a direction marker indicates a route to the silica mines up some steps to the right. Ignore these, continuing up the eastern bank, scrambling down a wall near a small fall. When the bank steepens, the path climbs to the right and then descends to the river at an open area where **gunpowder workings** can be seen on the far bank (see 'Gunpowder works,' Walk 32).

Continue upstream and begin to climb past a ruined building on the left to the first waterfall which has two tiers. The path climbs above it, crossing a steep-sided valley. There are striking iron-pigmented rocks below in the river. Eventually the path reaches a high point but do not descend where the path drops to river level before the river swings into a left-hand bend.

At the high point on the path is a steep, grassy, wooded slope leading up to the horizon. Make your way up this past an oak tree, passing a small rock outcrop on the right side. There is no clear path at first but keep on the arête of the hill meeting a path which zigzags up to a large oak tree on the left. From here continue due east to coniferous forestry on the right. Follow a low stone wall on the left which meets the track from Craig y Ddinas at the ruins of Cilhepste-fach.

Continue ahead, following the yellow arrow on the left and then white arrows to the left across deforested land. The track bears slightly right when it meets the Hepste Valley. ◄

The path soon comes to some large boulders which mark the start of a descent left down wooden steps to **Sgwd yr Eira.** These boulders are glacial erratics which were transported by ice from the north and then left behind when the ice melted and the glacier retreated. The path descends to a steep gully which formed due to a geological fault running through it which weakened the rock. This fault was also responsible for the original formation of the waterfall which has since retreated upstream.

Look carefully here to find orchids flowering in spring and summer.

SGWD YR EIRA

This is the most exciting to visit of all the falls in the Brecon Beacons National Park. It provides the unforgettable experience of walking behind a moving curtain of thundering water. The character of the fall is the result of the local geology. Notice when you stand behind the fall that your feet are on hard sandstone but that the rocks in a 1.5m recessed band at the base of the cliff are relatively weak, thinly bedded shales that crumble away easily. This band is very conspicuous

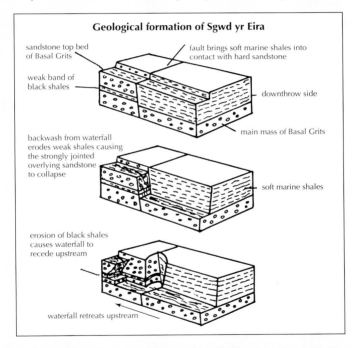

Geological formation of Sgwd yr Eira

sandstone top bed of Basal Grits

fault brings soft marine shales into contact with hard sandstone

weak band of black shales

downthrow side

main mass of Basal Grits

backwash from waterfall erodes weak shales causing the strongly jointed overlying sandstone to collapse

soft marine shales

erosion of black shales causes waterfall to recede upstream

waterfall retreats upstream

as it is covered in wet-loving vegetation. The rocks above are of a more resistant sandstone but are weakened by numerous bedding planes. The final massive band of sandstone which forms the protruding shelf over which the water tumbles is the strongest and so is the most resistant to collapse, resulting in the fall being thrown out spectacularly into space. ▶

The fall developed where a geological fault caused the river to flow from hard sandstone on to soft shales. Removal of the shales undermines the sandstone beds above causing the waterfall to migrate upstream, now over 70m from where the fault crosses the gorge. This point is marked by a gully in the southern side of the gorge which formed in response to weakening of the rocks by movement along the fault. This fall shares many characteristics in its formation with the famous Niagara Falls. Amazingly, the fall has frozen in severe winters. Adventurous canoeists have actually shot this fall and, for a short time, the record for the highest drop by canoe in Britain was held here.

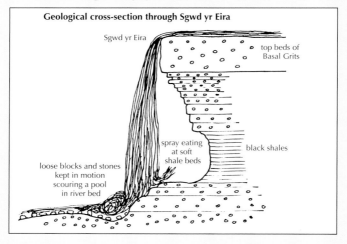

Geological cross-section through Sgwd yr Eira

Sgwd yr Eira

top beds of Basal Grits

spray eating at soft shale beds

black shales

loose blocks and stones kept in motion scouring a pool in river bed

After exploring behind the waterfall, return up the steps to the boulders and bear left along an obvious path following the top of the wooded gorge to a stile. A yellow National Park arrow directs you along the right of a fence past a warning sign concerning the dangers of the Waterfall Country. This waymarked path brings you back to the start in Penderyn.

Alternative route

Take the left turn signposted to the silica mines, down wooden steps to the river. Cross the river bridge by the silica mines, turn right and then climb up left onto the ridge through oak, beech and hawthorn woodland to a large concrete block on the right with metal stansions let into it. These concrete stansions are all that remains of an unusual aerial ropeway used to transport stone from the mine to level ground near to Craig y Ddinas. Don't take the steep path that drops to the river but swing left on the ridge and follow the path down through woodland and bracken to a lane. Continue down right to **Craig y Ddinas** and the car park.

Craig y Ddinas is a 50m-high **limestone cliff** of great geological significance, as the continuation of the Vale of Neath Disturbance runs through it. The contorted limestone strata here are the surface evidence of enormous crustal earth movements which took place along lines of weakness known as geological faults. The tilted limestone beds of the near-vertical face provide challenging rock routes, whereas the easy cliffs to its right are popular with beginners learning to climb and abseil. Legend claims that the rock is the final resting place of King Arthur and the Knights of the Round Table.

WALK 32
Ystradfellte Falls

Start	Coed y Rhaiadr Forestry Commission car park (SN918 103)
Map required	Central Map OL11
Distance	14km (8.7 miles)
Total ascent	Negligible

The Ystradfellte Waterfall Country has been famous for its natural beauty for many years. This varied route visits the spectacular waterfalls and steep wooded gorges of this area, taking in true ancient woodland, a rich industrial past and excellent geological and geomorphological features. It is quite a long walk along muddy and sometimes slippery river paths but there should be no difficulty in route finding if directions are carefully followed.

171

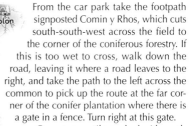

From the car park take the footpath signposted Comin y Rhos, which cuts south-south-west across the field to the corner of the coniferous forestry. If this is too wet to cross, walk down the road, leaving it where a road leaves to the right, and take the path to the left across the common to pick up the route at the far corner of the conifer plantation where there is a gate in a fence. Turn right at this gate.

Cross over a stile marked with a yellow National Park arrow, just after Carn y Crochan. Continue following the ditch on the left across a field with gorse, silver birch and alder to your left. On the right you can see the farm buildings of **Pentre-d'rysgoed**. Cross this field and over a stile, keeping the ditch on the left, where you pick up the farm track which after about 60m goes down to a gate with another yellow arrow.

Immediately through the gate turn left to the bank of the stream and regain the right of way with the old wall on the right. Shortly, join the farm track and continue down it to a large gate. Beyond this, keep on the track which crosses poor grazing land and runs through a gap in a wall at two solid fence posts.

Bear right, south-west, along the south side of the wall by field maple, mountain ash and hawthorn to the junction of several walls. You may be lucky enough to see curlew here. Head across the bracken-covered field ahead in a south-westerly direction to a junction of several collapsed stone walls. Continue in the same direction, following the wall which leads down the crest of the ridge in the direction of the Neath Valley. The wall more or less disappears but from here you will be able to see the boundary of the golf course. From this point, cut right to a stile in this wall at the apex of the course, marked by a small viewing tower.

Cross over the stile and proceed along the right of way with a stone wall to the right. From the most southerly tip of this path, before it bends to the right and into the valley, make for the spur of land between a golf tee and green where there are wooden electricity poles. Continue to a stile with a yellow waymarker and drop down the wooded spur, bearing sharply right to a stream on the right and so to some houses.

Turn left round the front of the houses and to the right is a sign to a picnic area. Cross the river by the bridge, below which is the confluence of the Mellte and the Sychryd rivers. Turn left with **Craig y Ddinas** straight ahead. On the left of the crag is an advised path sign, but just before the crag take a small path down to the left to the river bed where there is a sign for the gunpowder works.

Down to the left of the **Afon Mellte** and just beyond is a steep bank which divides the river from a large lagoon. Follow the path which drops to river level. The path passes through mainly hazel, birch and ash woodland (see 'Ancient Woodland,' Walk 30). It then climbs again, leaving a steep drop to the water below. ▸

About a kilometre from the crag is a weir where there is a steel cable crossing from a stilling well on the opposite bank. This is used to measure the rise and fall of the river. The path climbs steeply to the right, leaving the river and passing through beech woodland and beds of wild garlic. Look out for a disused mine adit on the right-hand side.

As you leave the wood the track divides. Take the left branch level with the river bed. The conifers ahead were planted just after the Second World War (see 'Changing Woodland,' Introduction). The path follows a bend in the river, arriving at some old workings represented by a stone wall and river race. Beyond is a wooden bridge built by Norwegians and on the right are steps up the hillside signposted to the silica mines. Another sign indicates gunpowder works across the bridge. Ignore these and continue along the river bed by a deep pool and scramble down to a weir below and onto the small island. This way is impassable when the river is in flood and a detour up and around to the right must be made, regaining the bank of the river further upstream. Continue along the

Further evidence of this area's industrial past can be seen on the opposite side of the river where there is a man-made sluice.

Wild garlic or ramsons

The best time to visit this area is early morning when no-one else is around. This is when the woods are full of birdsong and you have your best chance of seeing dippers, herons and other birds along the streamcourse.

path, now with an alder wood growing in a boggy area to your right, and cross a wooden stile. ◄

Shortly after the stile the river is forced into a much narrower channel with a number of small falls. Make a short detour here, dropping down left to explore these with a fine exposure of Millstone Grit in the opposite bank (see Walk 33). The dip of the rocks to the south is clearly evident here. Above are numerous disused workings. The path now climbs and then drops again to the river.

Old iron panels can be seen in the river bed and across on the opposite bank are numerous ruined stone buildings amongst conifers. Continue to old stone piers at a former bridging point. Explore this assortment of sluices and weirs, which once provided the power for the gunpowder works here.

GUNPOWDER WORKS

Alongside the Mellte was a gunpowder works which was unique in Wales at the time. The first owners were the Vale of Neath Powder Company but in 1862 Curtis and Harvey took over the works and eventually renamed it Nobels Explosives Company. In 1926 it became part of Imperial Chemical Industries Limited. The site was understandably chosen for its isolation, the river supplied power and the woodland was used for making charcoal. The site covered about 180 acres stretching for nearly two miles. This meant that any explosion could be contained.

The works are largely in ruins today but stonework and remnants of buildings can be seen, many of which have only three remaining walls as the fourth wall and roof were made of timber that would be blown off if an explosion occurred. The buildings were separated by banks of earth and many were whitewashed so that accumulation of gunpowder could be spotted easily. Workers wore special safety slippers made of leather and women were banned from wearing metal hairpins. Work commenced at 7.30 am and nothing likely to cause a spark could be taken into the buildings. The gunpowder produced here was principally used in coal mines and quarries, including the slate quarries of North Wales. The head of water that fed the water-wheels that powered the machinery was supplied via two weirs and a series of leats. Raw materials were hauled on a tramway by horses shod with copper shoes to prevent sparks.

From the weir, continue upstream past a small stone structure on the right to the first waterfall. At the entrance to the pond below the fall the river has breached a band of Millstone Grit and the water actually runs down the dipslope of the bedding plane. The waterfall just beyond has been formed by a resistant band of sandstone. Pass this fall up to the right, crossing a wide boulder-filled gully. There are good exposures in the right-hand wall of well-cleaved Millstone Grit. Leaving the gully, take the path that goes up to the right.

Rock Climbing on Craig y Ddinas

The gorge continues to narrow as you progress upstream, with a steep drop from the path to the river. Both sides of the valley are wooded (see 'Ancient Woodland,' Walk 30). Rounding the bend, the river straightens into a narrow channel with a number of small falls. The river then swings to the right around a spur of land. Eventually the path reaches a high point but do not descend where the path drops to river level. This is just before the river swings into a left-hand bend and the gorge further on soon becomes impassable. If you miss this point, retrace your steps to where the path reaches the crest of a small rise.

At the high point on the path there is a steep grassy wooded slope leading up to the horizon. Make your way up this past an oak tree, keeping a small rock outcrop on the right-hand side. There is no clear path at first but keep on the arête of the hill, meeting a path which zigzags upwards. From here there are excellent views north of the interlocking spurs of this valley.

Continue east along a flattish section to a large oak tree on the left. East from here, a path leads along the side of a ditch on the left to a broken-down wall along the edge of a conifer plantation. The path swings to the right (with the wall on the left) through a cutting in the forestry to the high-level path on the right which joins Sgwd yr Eira with Craig y Ddinas. Continue up the rise and cut off left at the route sign to the ruins of Cilhepste-fach.

Swing around the ruins and follow the wide path northwards. The path is parallel to the river which is well below. The Forestry Commission is attempting to regenerate oak woodland on the left of the path but has unfortunately decimated this area in previous years by draining the peat and heather moorland and planting alien conifers (see 'Coniferous Forestry,' Walk 20). To the south-west is the Neath Valley with the land massif on the left, the Rhigos, forming the northern rim of the South Wales coalfield. The rounded mountain straight ahead is Fan Nedd.

The path swings to the east and follows above the **Afon Hepste** to a group of large boulders and a footpath marker indicating Sgwd yr Eira to the left and Penderyn to the right. The sides of this gorge are very steep and, in fact, prevented the woodland here from being felled. This is an area of genuine ancient woodland, which means that this is a completely natural habitat which has not been interfered with by Man (see Walk 30). ◄

Drop steeply down wooden steps towards the river. Halfway down the track divides. Take the right descending path which crosses behind the falls. The gully you have just descended is where the geological fault runs, which was originally responsible for the creation of the fall. Passing behind the Sgwd yr Eira fall is one of the most memorable experiences in the National Park (see Walk 31).

On the far bank keep down at river level, ignoring the path that climbs the hillside by the steps. Soon you come across a series of cascades called the **Lower Cilhepste Falls.** This is an exciting place to explore and to discover how these falls were formed.

The group of four or five large boulders is a geological oddity as their rock type is not found in the National Park. They were, in fact, transported by glaciers during the Ice Age from much further afield and are known as glacial erratics.

LOWER CILHEPSTE FALLS

This part of the gorge is where the Afon Hepste plunges over 70m down a number of steps to reach the confluence with the Afon Mellte. The Hepste gorge has been left as a 'hanging valley' above the Mellte and these multiple cascades have been formed where the steepest gradient is found and where a geological fault crosses the gorge. This is the same fault which is responsible for Sgwd Isaf Clun-gwyn where it crosses the Mellte. The Mellte was able to 'capture' the Hepste as its valley is much lower than the Hepste. This triggered a period of rapid erosion in the Hepste which is at its most active at these falls. The gorge is known as Devil's Glen and is supposed to be inhabited by all manner of other-worldly folk including ghosts and fairies.

Strike up right, leaving the river path which soon becomes impassable. The path winds up in a zigzag past a rock boulder and a group of very tall beech trees on the left. There is a choice of either taking an easy route which avoids a steep descent and an exposed path or a more adventurous route.

EASY route: The easier option is to follow the main path which climbs above to the right to a spur above the

Sgwd Isaf Clun-gwyn

confluence of the Hepste and the Mellte where there is a notice 'Danger – Very steep rough slippery ground, deaths have occurred, take care'. This is near to a large prominent oak tree. Head north from the notice, keeping to the top edge of the gorge.

HARD route: If you are adventurous, and want to regain the bank of the river as soon as possible, keep left and contour round the spur on a shale path which drops down very steeply to the river. Use the trees and tree roots for safety here and arrive at the confluence of the Rivers Hepste and Mellte. Turn right (NW) up the River Mellte until the river bank becomes impassable and climb the spur on the right. Before reaching the top, take the path off to the left and traverse round the hillside, dropping to Sgwd y Pannwr. The path skirts just above the river and comes to a sign 'Danger – very steep rocky path'.

Rounding a right-hand bend in the gorge, you will hear the roar of a waterfall down in the gorge called **Sgwd y Pannwr**. The slope on the right eases and the path drops gently through woodland, across a Millstone Grit boulder field to the waterfall.

Continue upstream along the river bank to the waterfall **Sgwd Isaf Clyn-gwyn**. Just around the corner is another Millstone Grit boulder slope and beyond this is the most spectacular series of waterfalls in South Wales. Explore all the pools and cascades, savouring this very special place (to learn more about its formation see Walk 30).

On your way to the waterfall, look to your right where there is a flat boggy area with alder woodland. The steep cliffs on the opposite bank in springtime will be covered in primroses.

Climb steeply above the last fall to the right of two large sandstone bands. Either take a slightly airy path along a terrace between these two massive bands of rock. This soon joins the main gorge path. This exposed route provides an excellent aerial view of the fall below.

The massive sandstone band above to your right is a very important geological feature and is known as the 'twelve foot sandstone'. Note the 'mantel-shelf' that has formed at the base of this bed where the rock type changes to very weak, thinly bedded shales. This feature is responsible for many of the cascades in the Waterfall Country, none more noteworthy than Sgwd yr Eira.

Or, cut up above this rock outcrop to the main high-level path. Proceed along this, around a bend in the gorge, to the next waterfall, **Sgwd Clun-gwyn**.

Look carefully at some of the loose boulders here to find a clue as to how the fall originally formed. Some of the rock surfaces have been polished and scored with parallel grooves. These are called 'slickensides' and are formed when rocks grind together along a geological fault. These boulders are not, however, oriented in their original position when the earth movements occurred.

Climb to the gully that is in line with the waterfall. The geological fault that formed the fall runs through this. From here, either walk up to the wooden bridge, cross the river and follow the opposite bank down to the fall, or if the river level is low, descend to the river just above the fall and jump across at a narrow point. The fall can be explored by climbing down its right edge to a rocky ledge halfway down the fall. The deep pools above the fall are ideal for a refreshing dip on warm summer days. The ledge of the fall is a good place to learn more about its history (see 'Sgwd Clun-gwyn,' Walk 30).

From the top of the fall ascend the path up to the left through oak and hawthorn woodland. The track climbs more

Sgwd Clun-gwyn

179

steeply to an open area and a gate by the farmhouse of **Clungwyn**. Cross the stile and over sheep grazing land to the road. Turn left (S) and walk back to the start.

WALK 33

Afon Nedd and Afon Mellte

Start	Pont Mellin-fach car park (SN908 105)
Map required	Central Map OL11
Distance	13km (8 miles)
Total ascent	Negligible

This route travels northwards along the banks of the Afon Nedd to one of the most interesting and impressive natural features in the area – Pwll-y-rhyd cave. It then crosses a limestone plateau into the Ystradfellte Valley and descends the Afon Mellte past impressive waterfalls. The route is not well frequented, at least in its early stages, and can be quite difficult, especially in wet weather. There can be some problems in route finding as the path often leaves the river and the passage over the limestone plateau in the north requires good map reading. The geology of the valleys, moving from grit to limestone, is interesting and there is an Iron Age fort to the north.

Leave the car park to the north and cross over the bridge. Turn immediately left, cross over a stile and follow the path along the right bank of the stream signed to Pont Rhyd-y-cnau. The path drops to river level and, in a short distance, passes under a small cliff. This may be difficult when the river is in flood and the stones are slippery. In these conditions this section may be passed at a higher level. ◄

Look out for dippers and wagtails in the stream bed.

Eventually it becomes impossible to follow the path at river level and it skirts below the next set of crags climbing up to the top of the bank. Climb up to high level opposite this, or the more adventurous can follow the narrow path behind the holly. There is a pleasant plunging waterfall on the opposite bank. This is a spectacular wooded area with boulders covered in a variety of mosses. The closer you stay to the edge, the more exciting or dangerous the walk becomes. The river takes a contorted route through steep gorge walls with the odd small waterfall and deep pool. The banks of the river are covered mainly with hazel, ash, holly, rowan and sycamore (see 'Ancient Woodland,' Walk 30).

The right of way marked on the map runs across the top of the cliff but the walk is more interesting when the bank is followed as far as conditions will allow. Other tree species include silver birch and oak. The gorge walls were formed in the Millstone Grit and along this stretch you can see good examples of stratification.

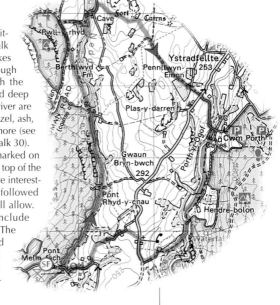

GEOLOGICAL ROCK FORMATIONS OF THE WATERFALL COUNTRY

Carboniferous limestone was formed in warm, often clear, shallow seas where corals, shellfish, brachiopods and crinoids (sea-lilies) were abundant. In fact, the skeletal remains of creatures such as these can make up much of the rock. The Devonian period ended when the southern flanks of St George's Land (see 'Geology of the Brecon Beacons,' Introduction) subsided, with the result that the sea, which was confined to an area south of the present Bristol Channel, advanced northwards. This marked the beginning of Carboniferous times when up to 4000ft of grey calcareous shales and massive limestones were deposited. These rocks are divisible into three groups, Lower Limestone Shales, Main Limestone and Upper Limestone Shales, which reflect the establishment, hiatus and waning of a major marine cycle. These stable conditions were interrupted by earth movements caused by approaching continents from the west and south in mid-Carboniferous times which lifted the southern flanks of St George's Land, resulting in a southward retreat of the sea. The rocks once laid down on the seabed were now exposed to erosion. ▶

181

Overlying the limestone is Millstone Grit which, in the Beacons, comprises in its lower layers massive white quartz conglomerates and sandstones, the Basal Grit. This group has very pure bands of over 99% quartz which were worked for firebrick (silica brick). The Millstone Grit represents a marked change in depositional conditions to estuaries of large rivers in which fast currents carried coarse material eroded from mountains to the north. Many of the beds show rapid lateral changes from fine silty muds to coarse sandstones, grits and conglomerates. These resistant layers are overlain by softer grey or blue shales and mudstones, the Middle Shales, which sometimes contain thin bands of coal. These shales are followed by massive beds of sandstone, known commonly by South Wales miners as the Farewell Rock, as they knew that workable coal bands were left behind once they had struck this distinctive geological marker.

This area is well populated with small woodland birds and heron are commonly seen along the river. Late April is a good time of the year to visit when all the woodland flowers are in bloom.

Follow your preferred route here, staying close to the river with a bit of scrambling across boulders and then strike up right to a stile. This is at grid line 11 on the map and there is a waterfall on the far river bank. Drop again to the river and continue north if water levels allow. Cross a small rivulet on the right and walk by a single-strand fence. ◄

Now and again fences have to be crossed by fairly rough stiles before coming to a sign to Pont Rhyd-y-cnau. Follow this to arrive at a bridge with a gate barring the route. Just below the bridge is a waterfall and there is a sloping block of Millstone Grit in the river bed which gives the true dip direction for the area. Skirt past the bridge without crossing and continue through deciduous forestry along the river bank. Ignore the wide track down from the right to the bridge. Dippers are quite common in the stream bed. Continue on the west bank to the rapids through oak woodland and cross a stile and a stream gully. Fifty metres further is an impressive stepped waterfall on the far bank, which is spectacular when frozen.

Parts of the banks are composed of grit and parts are of limestone. The trees on the river bank are covered in moss on the lower parts with a number of ferns growing from the trunks; these are called epiphytes. In the spring there is an abundance of woodland flowers including lesser celandine (*Ranunculus ficaria*), a yellow flower.

Immediately past these waterfalls, the path enters a narrow gorge, and there is a river pool with a limestone cliff beyond it called **Pwll Du**. The water here is extremely clear and flows out through the exit of the cave. This indicates that this pool is the resurgence of an underground cave system. Just after the pool, the path climbs up into a narrow gorge and up out of the right-hand side. Follow the path as it drops down below the crag. A short distance up from Pwll Du, the river swings to the right around a tall cliff. In the dry season you can traverse across the front of this, otherwise climb to the top. Above this point the resurgence of the river occurs. Water seeps out of the gravel-bed, having travelled underground leaving a dry river bed upstream. In spate, this phenomenon is obscured.

At the point where the dry river bed is between a narrow gorge, cut up right just before the crags on the path. Climb a grassy boulder incline up rock steps to large Millstone Grit boulders and up to the fence on the top of the hillside. Follow the path along the fence on the right. The path comes to a corner of the wire fence above which a stony track descends to the river. Follow this upstream to the bridge.

Cross the bridge to the left bank and climb the farm track through coppiced hazel, passing a ruined building on the right of the path. The path bends to the left into a gully. This is worth a quick visit because it is headed by a sink hole, over the lip of which fall several small streams which pass underground and eventually find their way down to the river. Below the sink hole turn north through an ungated gap in the fence and into a field. Walk up this, leaving a fence between you and the river far below in a deep gorge.

When ruined buildings come into view, head for these and follow the hawthorn hedge and the old wall to a stile. Cross this to the old farm buildings and up the track to join the Roman Road, **Sarn Helen**, at a sign which points back along this road and also back to Duffryn Nedd.

Follow Sarn Helen along the edge of the coniferous forestry until just before two gates. The hills ahead are Fan Nedd and the low bulk of Fan Gyhirych. A track leaves on the right. Follow this stony road down to a gate where it bends to the left. On the bend, turn right off the track and cut down the river bank southwards to **Pwll-y-rhyd** which is about 100m downstream. This is an incredible limestone sink hole, where

Pwll-y-rhyd, limestone sink hole

the river pours over its lip and disappears for about 200m underground. The river can be crossed with care in dry conditions and the opposite bank can be explored.

If the river has been crossed, continue northwards up the eastern bank above Pwll-y-rhyd. Otherwise proceed upstream along the western bank to the bridge. There is a choice of paths along the eastern bank, the lowest one passing below a cliff on rock steps in the river. This may need to be avoided in spate. The track now becomes sandy and arrives at a stile and bridge on the track you left before visiting Pwll-y-rhyd. There is a car park here.

Turn right up the tarmac track to a wider road and turn left by a sign for camping and caving. After about 150m cross a stile on the right of the road, at a sign to **Ystradfellte**. Strike south-east diagonally across the field to a stile and then continue to hawthorn trees on the horizon. From these, aim for the southern edge of the limestone **hill fort**, meeting and following a stone wall. The fort is situated on a limestone pavement. To the north east is Carnau Gwynion, a circular ceremonial site dating back to the Neolithic Period.

LIMESTONE PAVEMENT

Walk 33 crosses one of the most southerly limestone pavements in Britain. The characteristic appearance results from the limestone, calcium carbonate, being dissolved along joints by slightly acidic rainwater. The raised blocks are known as clints and the clefts as grikes. In the past, this area was wooded as the plants found in the grikes are typical woodland species. The deep grikes have a stable 'micro-climate' of low light levels and constant temperatures, characteristics of a woodland floor. Typical grike plant species include lily of the valley (*Convallaria majalis*), wall lettuce (*Mycelis muralis*), hard shield fern (*Polystichum aculeatum*), hairy rock-cress (*Arabis hirsuta*), brittle bladder fern (*Cystopteris fragilis*), limestone fern, globe flower (*Trollius europaeus*) and unusual limestone pavement species such as common cow-wheat (*Melampyrum pratense*), cowslip (*Primula veris*) and zigzag clover (*Trifolium medium*). Rarities include yellow archangel (*Galebdolon luteum*), found only in Wales, narrow-leaved bitter cress (*Cardamine impatiens*) and local drifts of mossy saxifrage (*Saxifraga hypnoides*). Dense hazel scrub is found in places with hawthorn, blackthorn, guelder-rose, dog rose, stone bramble, ivy, elder and honeysuckle.

Limestone pavement, Carnau gwynion

Cross over the stile and turn right, down the valley, to shortly meet a drovers' road. Follow this through an area of shake holes to the prominent Scots pines and then down the gully to meet the main road. These pines mark the route of this old drovers' road (see 'Drovers,' Walk 27). Cross this and descend the road to **Porth yr Ogof**. The valley north of the road bridge can be explored by dropping down a steep path from the car park. The river goes underground through Porth yr Ogof but don't be tempted to follow it as the cave has extremely deep and fast watercourses.

From the car park, cross the bridge and turn left (S) over a stile, following the direction sign for Cavers, and wander between limestone boulders and between two fenced-off sink holes, in the depths of which can be heard the rushing river. The path descends to the eastern bank as the river emerges into a limestone gorge. The route descends to the river here but an easier option stays above. This is Blue Pool, the resurgence of the **Afon Mellte**.

The path becomes easier and crosses above an open grassy area where the river is wider and more peaceful, and then widens and runs close to the river through woodland. Cross a rivulet and the path meanders and climbs above the river, which has narrowed with rapids. There is a swing gate and the path is at river level. Cross another small rivulet to a second swing gate and so to a sandy path curving left around the bend in the river to a wooden bridge with waymark arrows.

Cross the bridge and follow the clear path south to just above **Sgwd Clun-gwyn** waterfall. You can detour down to the fall and explore it by climbing down the right edge to a rocky ledge halfway down the fall (see Walk 30). Rejoin the path and ascend south-west following the track through bracken and oak and hawthorn woodland. The track climbs steeply at first to an open area and a gate by the renovated farmhouse of **Clun-gwyn**. Cross the stile and up the track to the road.

Turn right (N) over a cattle grid and after 200m there is a shop and garage. Beyond is a small church (**Capel Hermen**) opposite which cross a stile, signed to Heol-fawr. Strike across the field towards the farm hidden in the trees, and cross a waymarked stile turning right to a gate. Turn left on the road to **Heol-fawr Farm**.

Follow the waymark arrows along a permitted footpath through woodland and then along a stream to the road. Turn right and then just after the entrance to **Glyn-mercher-isaf**

Farm take the footpath on the right, across some fields and back to the road. Turn right down to the bridge and back to the start.

Sgwd Isaf Clun-gwyn

6 THE BLACK MOUNTAIN (MYNYDD DU)

Sinc Giedd

WALK 34
Carmarthen Fans and Glacial Cwms

Start	Car park, head of the Sawdde Valley (SN800 238)
Map required	Western Map OL12
Distance	14km (8.75 miles)
Total ascent	637m (2089ft)

This is the shortest route to the highest summits in Mynydd Du and although short in distance it is packed full of interest, from the mythical stories associated with Llyn y Fan Fach to spectacular glacial features. This walk is in the Fforest Fawr Geopark.

Head up the obvious track with the **Afon Sawdde** down on your right. The ground you are walking on comprises the Senni Beds that change to the Brownstones at the fish farm. The highest summits are capped by the resistant Plateau Beds (see 'Geology of the Brecon Beacons,' Introduction). The track arrives at a small **trout farm** after 0.9km and the path bypasses it on the left.

Take time to watch the trout jumping in the **holding pools**. In 1994, the Llynyfan Hatchery was

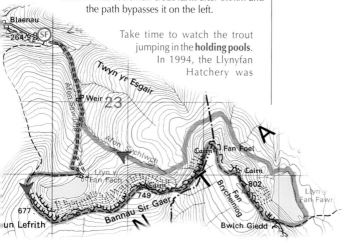

opened to rear Towy and Cleddau Salmon in mitigation for Llyn Brianne and Llys-y-fran Reservoirs. Brown trout from the upper Teifi are also reared for restocking rivers and stillwaters.

Straight ahead are the northern slopes of the Carmarthen Fan. The track continues to a **weir** and ford. Ignore the turning to the left later on and, after 1km, the glacial lake of **Llyn y Fan Fach** is reached. The lake was dammed in the early part of the 20th century. From 1918 until 1993 the lake was used as a direct water supply reservoir for Llanelli. It is bounded by moraines which are most obvious on the left side. There is an emergency stone refuge which has an open-hearth fire.

MYTHICAL LAKE

Llyn y Fan Fach is the setting for the legend of the Lady of the Lake. A young man used to take his cattle to graze on the local hills when he came across the lady sitting on the water combing her hair. He admired her beauty and offered her bread and cheese but she refused saying, 'Unbaked is thy bread I will not have thee.' She refused him on a second occasion but on his third visit she accepted his gift and agreed to marry him. Her dowry was sheep, cattle, goats and horses but she warned him, 'Strike me without cause three times and you shall lose me.' They lived together and had a family but alas he did strike her three times, though not with malice, and she returned to the lake with all her animals. She later appeared to her sons and taught them about herbs with medicinal uses. They went on to become the famous physicians of Myddfai and a study of their 13th-century recipes shows that Welsh medicine was far in advance of that in most of Europe. Directions were given as to the quantities and methods of preparation of the ingredients, which was most unusual at that time.

Llyn y Fan Fach from Bannau Sir Gaer

Turn west up a well-marked path to the skyline up a fairly gentle slope curving to the south to a high point, **Bannau Sir Gaer.** From here there are spectacular views down to Llyn y Fan Fach and north to the Usk Reservoir and into Mid-Wales. Continue round the ridge of Bannau Sir Gaer and up to the cairn at Picws Du.

From here the path drops steeply to the col at Bwlch Blaen Twrch where the **Afon Sychlwch** tumbles down to the north. Take the path east to the summit of **Fan Foel** and follow the ridge to the trig point on **Fan Brycheiniog.** This is the highest point of the range at 802m. There are spectacular views down to another glacial lake, Llyn y Fan Fawr and of the Brecon Beacons to the east.

FAN FOEL

The summit is the site of an early Bronze Age (2000BC) round barrow that was excavated in June 2004. A stone curb defined the edge of the barrow, which had a central cist comprising a stone-box made from stone slabs. A cremation deposit was found in this and examination of the bone identified the presence of an adult, a young child and an infant, as well as two pigs and possibly a dog. A second cremation contained the remains an adult and a juvenile. A crushed pottery vessel from the central cist probably contained food and a triangular-shaped flint knife. There would have been a mound formed by peat and turf covering the cist.

Fan Foel and Fan Brycheiniog from Picws Du

Continue along the ridge to **Bwlch Giedd** where you turn left and drop down to **Llyn y Fan Fawr**.

Follow the eastern edge of the lake and traverse at the base of the cliffs to where the path drops down from Fan Foel. Continue in a westerly direction and then swing southwards, keeping at the base of the escarpment, to where you meet the path coming down from the ridge above at Pant y Bwlch. The sinuous linear mound you can see is a glacial moraine at the bottom of the cliff.

Keep following the base of the northern cliffs of Bannau Sir Gaer towards Llyn y Fan Fach. When the track divides, take the right-hand path (NW), parallel with the water-course down on the right, until it reaches a stone-lined channel which diverts part of the Afon Sychlwch into Llyn y Fan Fach. Cross this and follow the path to a ford at the weir above the trout farm, again with the stream on your right. From here, retrace your footsteps to the start.

WALK 35
Nant Pedol and Drysgol

Start	Llandeilo Road bridge across Nant Pedol (SN691 141)
Map required	Western Map OL12
Distance	5.6km (3.5 miles)
Total ascent	263m (2089ft)

A short walk in one of the remotest areas of the National Park. The route follows a section of gorge in Cwm Pedol which has ancient woodland and a beautiful stream. A pleasant walk through upland pasture leads to an easy ascent of Drysgol from where there are fine views.

Start at the bridge over the stream, **Nant Pedol**, on the Llandeilo Road. Facing upstream, take the track on the left through a gate signposted to Cwm Pedol. Walk up the track to the Welsh waterworks where you cross a stile and into mixed deciduous woodland.

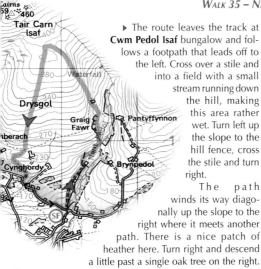

▶ The route leaves the track at **Cwm Pedol Isaf** bungalow and follows a footpath that leads off to the left. Cross over a stile and into a field with a small stream running down the hill, making this area rather wet. Turn left up the slope to the hill fence, cross the stile and turn right. The path winds its way diagonally up the slope to the right where it meets another path. There is a nice patch of heather here. Turn right and descend a little past a single oak tree on the right. The route passes through substantial areas of bilberry and heather. Continue past three oak trees on the right to a junction. Take the path to the left that runs across the slope in the direction of a farm barn on the opposite side of the valley. Do not take the path that descends to the stream and wooden bridge below.

The path enters pretty oak woodland with the valley side dropping steeply down to the stream below and the understorey carpeted in flowers in the spring (see 'Ancient woodland,' Walk 30 and 'Birdlife,' Introduction). Nant Pedol has cut this gorge through the Lower Coal Measures that comprise mudstones with coal seams. Drysgol is formed from the Farewell Rock and the higher mountains from the Basal Grit (see 'Geology of the Brecon Beacons,' Introduction and 'Geological rock formations of the Waterfall Country,' Walk 33).

Follow the waymarked path along the western side of Cwm Pedol. The route takes a track just to the right of a **ruined stone cottage** and soon afterwards crosses the hill fence. Turn right and follow an indistinct path that brings you to where the hill fence drops to the stream below. Continue diagonally upwards following the edge of the wet boggy area on your right. Eventually, you reach a stream gully. Do not

Keep an eye out for birds of prey during the walk. Buzzards, red kite and kestrels are a common sight here.

193

Cwm Pedol

cross this but follow the bank to the ridge above. There are fine views to the south-west down the Amman Valley and to Gower on the horizon.

Turn left (S). The open moorland here is covered with heather, ling, bilberry, purple moor grass and bog cotton.

The National Park Authority are actively managing this habitat as the heather is infested with heather beetle and has become too old and degenerate to benefit wild-life or livestock. Patches are burnt to create a 'mosaic' habitat of different ages of heather stands. The air is full of the sound of singing skylarks in the spring (see 'Birds of the Mountains,' Walk 22).

As you descend the slope, look out for three trees on the open hillside. Keep these to your left and cross the hill fence through a kissing gate. Follow the path down to where it meets a gravel road and turn right to the road. Turn left and back to the start.

WALK 36

Sinc Giedd and Bannau Sir Gaer

Start	Pont Haffes (SN845 165)
Map required	Western Map OL12
Distance	20.5km (12.7 miles)
Total ascent	744m (2415ft)

A classic walk that explores the heart of Mynydd Du giving a real sense of mountain wilderness and a true taste of the nature of this remote upland massif. The route meanders through a moonscape of shake holes with a visit to where a stream disappears underground at a swallow hole, Sinc Giedd. This contrasts with the return route that follows the spectacular ridge of Bannau Sir Gaer. This walk should only be attempted in good visibility, because the path is ill-defined in one open upland section.

Start at the bridge Pont Haffes where the A4067 crosses the River Tawe. Looking upstream, take the gate on the right marked with a sign 'Danger crossing river in flood' and continue along the road to **Carreg Haffes Farm**. Cross over the stile and follow the track around to the right to another stile on the left. Continue straight ahead over another stile and across a field, keeping the fence on your left. Follow the blue bridleway arrows and cross over a stile at the end of the fence along a path on the edge of some woodland where you may see some llamas. The path brings you into **Cwm Haffes**.

Cross over the stile and follow the stream for a short distance on the right-hand side. Cross over the small first steam and walk diagonally over an island covered in gorse to where there are some reasonable stepping stones to cross the main stream when it is not in spate. There is a lovely view up to the right of the boulder-strewn Haffes river valley. The base of the Carboniferous limestone runs along the high right bank wall of this steep valley (see 'Geology of the Brecon Beacons,' Introduction; 'Geology of the Waterfall Country,' Walk 33).

If this is not safe to cross, retrace your steps back to the road, cross over the road bridge and walk south-westwards down the valley. Turn right after the **Shire Horse Centre** and then right again. Follow the footpath signs to bring you into the Haffes Valley to where you join the route again. Straight ahead is an old quarry track which leads diagonally up the hillside to the left.

There are excellent views down the Swansea Valley to Craig-y-Nos Castle which belonged to the celebrated opera diva Adelina Patti. On the right is the entrance to Dan-yr-Ogof, an extensive underground cave system that is open to the public. Beyond is the extensively quarried profile of the Cribarth (see 'Cribarth,' Walk 38).

Ignore the track which leaves on the right to some old quarry workings. Continue with the Swansea Valley down to your left. The hill fence then bends down to the left near the highest point of the quarry track. At this point, take the path, not marked with a finger post, which heads in the direction of a rocky outcrop on the summit of the hill to the west. There is a solitary tree sticking out of a rock outcrop on the right.

The path swings around to the right (N) and runs parallel with the rock outcrop and then gradually swings back to the west, leaving the outcrop to the left (S). It then becomes quite distinct and runs parallel with the Haffes Valley.

The route meanders between shake holes and outcrops of Carboniferous limestone forming a classic 'karstic' landscape (see Walk 31), with good views of the summits and ridges of Fan Hir and Fan Foel in the distance off to the right which are formed from the resistant grits and conglomerates of Old Red Sandstone (see 'Old Red Sandstone,' Walk 18). These form the route for the return part of the walk.

Along this path you will come across a pool on your left and then afterwards, on the right is a large upland peat bog, Waun Fignen Felen, below which is an extensive limestone cave system.

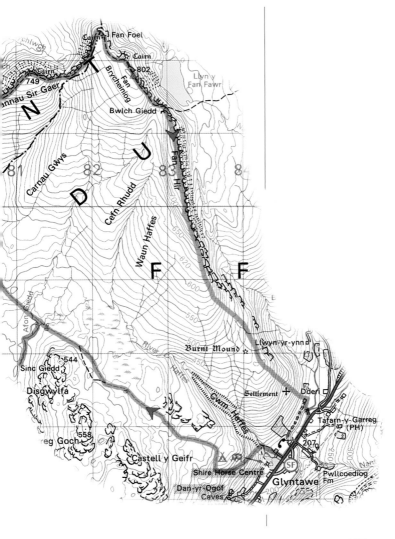

SHAKE HOLES

The numerous shake holes characteristic of Mynydd Du are depressions caused by the overlying Millstone Grit being undermined by the collapse of cavern roofs in the underlying Carboniferous limestone. Also known as sink holes or doline, they are bowl, cone or well shaped depressions in limestone-dominated areas. Karst topography is characterised by sink holes, cave systems and a lack of surface streams. Sink holes usually form where there is underground movement of water through caves or rock joints. Rainwater, being naturally mildly acidic, dissolves the limestone causing voids to be formed below the land surface. Sink holes are formed when these voids or caves collapse. They frequently provide access to cave systems or sub-surface streams and rivers.

Tawe Valley and Fan Gihirych

You may see some odd objects in the boggy area. These are to do with an innovative project, Black to Green, whose aim is to conserve and revegetate 15 hectares using mainly locally generated gorse mulch that contains a seedbank of acid grassland species. At first glance this remote bog appears to be of little interest but at the start of the Holocene it was an open lake surrounded by woodland and a watering place for wild animals. This led to its use as a station for Mesolithic hunters.

The bridleway descends down to Pwll y Cig. At this point, cross over a small stream, turn left leaving the track and follow the river valley (S). There are many boulders of Millstone Grit lying on the surface which have numerous large white quartz pebbles. Keep to the left bank on the higher ground until you reach the point where the stream disappears underground at **Sinc Giedd**.

The stream flows beneath this cliff of the Llandyfan Limestone during wet periods. The Giedd Valley is eroded along a north–south geological fault but the water that disappears here does not continue underground to feed the Afon Giedd but joins the Mazeways series in the Dan-yr-Ogof cave system 3km away as the crow flies. There have been many attempts by cavers to connect the sink holes in this area with Dan-yr-Ogof cave but these have so far been unsuccessful.

Cross over the valley below the cliff and make your way back to where you left the bridleway. The path becomes very indistinct after Pwll y Cig so care has to be taken in route finding. Continue north-west, crossing another small stream and up the hillside onto a grassy area. On the right is the high ground and the path splits just before this. Take the right-hand fork which heads just to the left of the hillock ahead. You come to the crest of the slope with the summit on the right and the track becomes clear again and drops down to the main stream gully below, with a large expanse of bog down to the left.

A ford is marked on the map but there is no evidence of this on the ground. Cross the stream at a convenient point and this may involve walking some distance upstream if the water level is high. Head up the slope and cross another stream, **Nant Lluestau**, and then up to the rocky crags above. Cross **Waun Lefrith** and finally gain the ridge and summit of **Bannau Sir Gaer.** Turn right (E) and follow the ridge to Picws Du.

There are fine panoramic views from here on a clear day of Plinlimon to the north, the Preseli Hills to the west, the Devon coast and Gower to the south and the Black Mountains to the east. A circular **cairn**, 19.5m in diameter by 1m high crowns the summit and this is probably a prehistoric funerary monument. Down below is the mythical lake Llyn y Fan Fach (see 'Mythical lake,' Walk 34).

A fine collection of unusual plants can be found where the sandstone is rich in lime in the crags above Llyn y Fan Fawr. These include mossy and burnet saxifrage, great burnet and roseroot as well as green spleenwort.

Fan Brycheniog from Fan Hir

The glacial cirques of Llyn y Fan Fawr and Llyn y Fan Fach are among the finest in South Wales with a further two cwms found to the east at Pwll yr Henllyn and Pany y Bwlch. Their associated Loch Lomond Stadial moraines can be seen clearly from the ridge above.

Descend to the col Bwlch Blaen Twrch, climb the ridge to the summit of **Fan Foel** and continue to the trig point on **Fan Brycheiniog.** There are excellent views to the east of the highest summits in the Brecon Beacons, Pen y Fan and Corn Du, and of the Black Mountains to the left of these. Down below is Llyn y Fan Fawr. To the north lie the Usk Reservoir and Mynydd Epynt. The cairn on Fan Foel is a round barrow (see 'Fan Foel,' Walk 34). ◄

Descend to Bwlch Giedd and climb again to **Fan Hir**. The origin of the linear ridge, Fan Fechan, at the base of the cliff is something of an enigma. It is over 20m high in places and comprises recycled fragments of Old Red Sandstone, possibly on a subdued bedrock ridge base in part. Two different modes of formation have been proposed. The first is that it is a glacial moraine and the second is that it is a protalus or nivation ridge (see Walk 25).

Follow the ridge and path to the hill fence and cross the stile at Ty Henry. Follow the path with the stone wall on your left and through the wall and then straight ahead. The path runs between two fields and then comes to the river. Turn right and follow the path along to the river, over the bridge and to the road. Turn right and take the road back to the start.

WALK 37
Afon Twrch

Start	New Tredegar Arms Public House, Cwm Twrch Uchaf, A4068 (SN757 113)
Map required	Western Map OL12
Distance	14.7km (9.2 miles)
Total ascent	496m (1628ft)

This route explores the finest valley in Mynydd Du. A tranquil river walk is followed by spectacular gorge scenery and a challenging wilderness section in the heart of the upland massif. A wide range of interests are catered for and highlights include its interesting archaeological and geological features. Route finding can be challenging in poor weather and this route is recommended only in good conditions.

With the pub behind you, cross the road and turn left in front of a row of terraced houses. The road becomes a track and the right of way makes a short detour left before turning right through a kissing gate. Turn left back onto the flat track. This is a disused tramway which used to bring limestone down from quarries in the hills. Keep a watch for grey heron in the river, the **Afon Twrch**, below.

Continue on the east side of the river taking the right unsigned track at a fork. Cross a wooden stile and a second stile as you approach the river bank. There are some cast metal sleeper shoes to be found. The track briefly meets a road at **Bryn-Henllys Bridge** on the left. Cross the road to continue along the eastern bank. At a small weir there is a picnic stop and stone shelter.

Cwm Twrch translates as 'Valley of the Wild Boar' and derives from the '**twrch trwyth**', a mythical wild boar of Arthurian legend which is also found in the ancient tales of the Mabinogion in early Welsh literature. There are several variations on this tale. One of King Arthur's tasks was to rid the western Brecon Beacons of the pack of wild boars that were terrorising the people. He chased the boars from Dyfed eastward towards Powys. It was on the Black Mountain that he picked up a large stone and hurled it at the pack, killing its leader on the edge of the valley near Craig-y-Fran Gorge. The big boar's body rolled down the valley and into the river, now known as the Afon Twrch.

Cross the river on the wooden bridge and just ahead is an impressive brick chimney and on the right an extensive rock exposure. Turn right and follow the path in-between the fence and the river, ignoring the two metal gates in the fence, and then cross where indicated by the waymark arrow. Shortly afterwards is an interesting rock outcrop of resistant sandstone beds and weaker shales (see 'Geology of the Brecon Beacons,' Introduction). A little further on is a well-preserved brick **chimney** and below it three large **limestone kilns**.

This area is known as the **Llosgi carreg** or **Burning Rock** and was the site of a kiln in use until the 1880s to produce lime for Ynyscedwyn Iron Works and later for the nearby brickworks. A rail incline ran due north from here up to the limestone quarries on Cefn Carn Fadog. It is thought that there were once two chimneys on this site and a further one on the hill above. Their original function is unclear but they were an essential part of the engine houses that either powered the incline, hauled coal from the mine or provided ventilation for underground mine workings.

Disused workings in Cwm Twrch

Continue along the path in front of the kilns and then up a small incline in the direction of a rock outcrop on the hillside ahead. Go through a kissing gate and take the path that climbs diagonally up the slope. In the river bed below, you can see the dip or slope of the sedimentary rocks being the same as the hillside you are walking on.

Turn left and follow the boundary wall around **Cyllie Farm**, ignoring an obvious track on the left and enter the open hillside beyond the farm buildings in a boggy area. Cross this and bear right and follow the path parallel with the river valley. There is a very narrow path below you which runs just along the top of the cliffs in places but this is very precarious. The gorge here is one of the finest in Wales, with superb views of the woodland clinging to the steep valley sides and of the deeply incised watercourse (see 'Ancient woodland,' Walk 32).

Continue following the river valley northwards, passing a derelict ruin on your right. Just after this, you come across a deep drainage ditch which leads to a stream gully. Cross this and drop down to the stream and follow the bank to where there is a narrow gorge and waterfalls. A tributary coming down on the opposite hillside has a fine waterfall. This is one of the remotest and wildest areas of Wales. Numerous upland and stream birds will be encountered.

Continue following the stream as the terrain allows, as some areas can be boggy. The Basal Grit boulder field on the valley sides has excellent areas of inaccessible bilberry and shows what the rest of the upland areas would be like without grazing animals. The valley side steepens on the eastern side and culminates in the resistant crags of **Tyle Garw**. Look out for the large spring called Ffrydiau Twrch that emerges from the western valley side. The route can be cut short by fording the stream at any suitable point and climbing up to Tyle Garw. Otherwise, continue upstream until the northern slope of Tyle Garw drops down to the stream at a meander.

Cross the stream and ascend the ridge in a southerly direction. The col down to the right is Bwlch Ddeuwynt, Gap of the Two Winds. From the summit ridge of Tyle Garw, head south and onto the ridge of land that separates the Twrch Valley from the **Gwys Fach** to its rounded summit. There are fine panoramic views to the north of the desolate heart of Mynydd Du and beyond to the high ridges of Bannau Sir

Gaer, Fan Foel and Fan Hir. The distinctive crinkled profile of Cribarth is to the east (see 'Cribarth,' Walk 38).

Afon Twrch near Tyle Garw

Descend the path (SW) and cross over a collapsed stone wall and follow this downslope on your right. Cross another wall and shortly afterwards the path finishes near a **standing stone**. From the stone, continue in the same direction to a track, turn left and continue SSW. Ahead on the left is the corner of a conifer plantation.

Leave the track after you cross a second boggy area and cut across the moorland to the corner of the forest. Follow the fence to a gate and go through this keeping to the main track and turn right just before the river bridge. This track follows the Gwys Valley down to **Tir-y-gof Bridge**. Take the bridleway just before the bridge and continue along the wide track. Turn left at a cross-roads of paths and then right to follow the bank of the river. The main track is joined again and this leads to a bridge. Cross this and follow the track down to the main road. Turn right and back to the start.

WALK 38
Henrhyd Falls and River Tawe

Start	Ynyswen A4067 (SN831 128)
Map required	Western Map OL12
Distance	7km (4.4 miles)
Total ascent	122m (400 ft)

A low-level walk along a spectacular wooded gorge with the highest waterfall in South Wales at its head. Owned and managed by the National Trust, the woodland is of special note and the humid habitat supports a wide variety of damp-loving species. A cross-country traverse then brings you to an impressive section of the River Tawe.

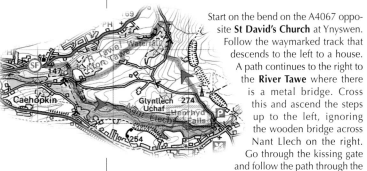

Start on the bend on the A4067 oppo-site **St David's Church** at Ynyswen. Follow the waymarked track that descends to the left to a house. A path continues to the right to the **River Tawe** where there is a metal bridge. Cross this and ascend the steps up to the left, ignoring the wooden bridge across Nant Llech on the right. Go through the kissing gate and follow the path through the woodland along the bank of the stream to the road.

Turn right and then leave the road to the left, cross a stile and take the path that leads along the left bank of **Nant Llech**. You soon reach the bank of the river where you have a good view of the rock strata that tilt or dip upstream creating small waterfalls, and you can appreciate why Nant Llech means 'rock-slab stream'.

The woodland on the southern bank of the gorge comprises mainly large single-stemmed trees that

*Henrhyd Waterfall frozen
in the winter of 2009*

have never been felled, whereas on the northern bank where you are walking the trees are multi-stemmed as they have been **coppiced**. This harvesting technique involves felling the tree near to its base and allowing it to grow back again. The drier upper slopes have sessile oak that can thrive in poor acidic soils. As you move closer to the stream the soils become wetter and more nutrient-rich and ash and alder are found. Wych elm and small-leaved limes also thrive here, indicating that this is ancient woodland (see 'Ancient Woodland,' Walk 30). Look out for damp-loving vegetation growing on the rocks, boulders and tree branches as Graig Llech is a Site of Special Scientific Interest for its wide range of rare mosses, ferns, lichens and liverworts.

An unusual sound you may hear are whoops of howler monkeys in the nearby primate sanctuary that gives the gorge a rather surreal atmosphere of a tropical jungle.

The path meets a track coming down from the left. Turn right continuing along the gorge to a wooden bridge. Do not cross but continue along the left side of the valley. You soon come to a ruined stone building, Melin-llech, which was once a **woollen mill**. The gorge is home to a variety of woodland and stream birds. Keep an eye out for pied flycatchers, dippers and kingfishers. ◄

After a while, you come to a National Trust sign for **Sgwd Henrhyd** and a wooden bridge. Continue to a kissing gate and the path then drops to the river where there is a 3m-high waterfall, again formed by a bedding plane in the rock. Take care traversing this as the rock can be slippery, and scramble back to the path again further up on the left.

The path meets a track coming down the valley side from the left which comes from the car park. Bear right here and to a wooden bridge across the main river from where, in the winter, you have a glimpse of the fall further up the gorge. Ascend the wooden steps on the other side to reach the waterfall on the right bank.

The waterfall has a vertical drop of 28m, making it the highest in South Wales. Earth movements 300 million years ago along a geological fault brought the hard sandstone of the Farewell Rock adjacent to softer, easily eroded Coal Measure shales which normally lie above. The water has worn away the soft shales at a faster rate than the sandstone, resulting in a step in the river bed.

During the past few thousand years, the size of the step has increased as the shale at the base of the waterfall is worn away and the overhanging Farewell Rock has collapsed to produce a spectacular gorge and high waterfall.

These soft shales make Nant Llech a famous location for their rich Westphalian fossil fauna. Also at this locality is the rarely found Astel Coal, a thin coal (30cm) that marks the start of the productive Coal Measures (see 'Geology of the Brecon Beacons,' Introduction).

Retrace your steps back to the bridge and follow the track that sweeps back on itself out of the gorge and to the car park. Turn left along the tarmac road to a communications tower on a bend. Two footpath signs are marked here. Take the one on the left that heads in the direction of the Cribarth mountain on the opposite side of the Tawe Valley. Cross the field heading for stile in the fence just to the left of an electricity post. Just before this cross over a boggy area via a boardwalk. Now head upslope to the right end of a row of trees.

Crossing over to the Tawe Valley towards Cribarth

CRIBARTH

This mountain, known locally as the 'Sleeping Giant' owing to its profile when seen from down-valley, was extensively quarried in the 19th century. The ridge runs along the 'Cribarth Disturbance', an ancient fault line in the Earth's crust, which manifests itself here as a couple of tight anticlinal folds in the rock. It is flanked by steeply dipping beds of gritstone and an area of rottenstone to the north. The latter is a unit of sandy limestone found at the contact between the limestone and Millstone Grit and was quarried and used as an abrasive and polish in the copper and tinplate industries of South Wales.

Do not go through the gate but keep the fence on your left and follow this to a wooded stream gully and down to the road. Turn right and follow the road to an old church on the right. Take the waymarked path on the left before the bridge. The track divides after 25m. Take the right fork where you will see a yellow footpath arrow on a post. This brings you to the edge of a steep cliff with the **Tawe river** below. There are excellent views from here of the valley and an impressive stretch of river rapids.

Follow the path along the top of the cliff, taking great care, to where a small stream runs down from the left. Just after you cross this, a yellow arrow shows the footpath turning left away from the edge of the cliff. Shortly afterwards you come to a barbed-wire fence. Turn right and then cross over a stile and right again between two fences, walk along a small streamway and through a gate where there is a stony track. This becomes a wide grassy area between two stone walls and brings you to a stile. Once you cross this, do not take the track to the farm, **Glyn-llech Isaf**, but keep the fence on your left to a gap in the trees where a bridge crosses a stream.

Turn left along a track and then right along a line of trees and a fallen down stone wall that mark an old field boundary that you keep on your left. In the fence ahead there is a yellow waymark arrow and a farm building just to the right. Cross the stile and follow the path with the moss-covered wall now on your right. Cross over a further two stiles and a gate and follow the track that leads to the road. Turn right down the hill and retrace your route to the start.

WALK 39

Cwm Sawdde and Garreg Las

Start	Pont Aber on the A4069 Llangadog to Brynamman (SN738 226)
Map required	Western Map OL12
Distance	14km (8.6 miles)
Total ascent	495m (1624ft)

A surprise awaits at the beginning of this route when a steep wooded gorge with a waterfall is discovered just after leaving the road. The route then follows the western side of Cwm Sawdde and height is gradually gained to reach the summit of Godr Carreg Las. There are impressive views to the east of Bannau Sir Gaer, to the south of the Amman Valley, and to the north of the Towy Valley. Route finding in the upland parts of this route can be difficult in low visibility but a low-level alternative is available if weather conditions are poor.

Start to the right of the bridge at Pont Aber at the confluence of the **Afon Sawdde** and the **Afon Clydach**, just south of the tea rooms. Cross the stile marked with a National Park yellow

Bannau Brycheiniog from Garreg Las

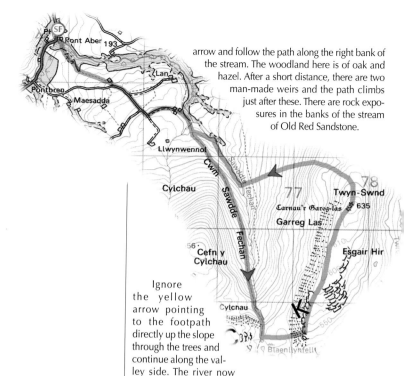

arrow and follow the path along the right bank of the stream. The woodland here is of oak and hazel. After a short distance, there are two man-made weirs and the path climbs just after these. There are rock exposures in the banks of the stream of Old Red Sandstone.

Ignore the yellow arrow pointing to the footpath directly up the slope through the trees and continue along the valley side. The river now runs in a deep gorge cut through the steeply tilted succession of Silurian and Ordovician sandstones and mudstones. The gorge swings away to the north at an impressive waterfall. At this point the path ends. Retrace your steps a little to the corner of a barbed-wire fence on the right. Follow this until you get to a wooden stile after about 50m.

Cross the stile and head across the boggy field, keeping the woodland on your left to a gate with a yellow arrow. Go through this, turn immediately left and cross another stile. Turn right and head for a solitary oak tree in the field ahead. Cross the field in the direction of the farm to a gate with a yellow arrow on the right. Go through the gate and turn right across the field where there is a gate in the fence on the left. Do not go up to the gate at the top of the field. Turn right and to the stile in the fence where you meet the road.

Turn left up the road. Shortly afterwards ignore the sign to Pentwyn on the right and continue up the road straight ahead. Where the metalled road ends, turn left along a farm track to **Neuadd Fach**. Go through the gate into the farmyard and continue on the bridleway to the **Sawdde** stream running in the narrow gorge below. This is a pretty area with oak woodland covering the valley sides.

Cross the ford and take the track sweeping up to the right and then left. The bridleway is quite indistinct but cross the boggy field to a gate in the hill fence marked with a blue arrow. The path is difficult to follow but head along the valley side and soon a distinguishable route appears where there is a slight break in the slope. This is a good opportunity to note the return route, which follows the ridge on the opposite side of the valley and then drops down the valley side to the river above the hill fence, avoiding awkward boulder fields and boggy areas.

Continue contouring along the valley side until you meet the stream. Do not cross but continue following the watercourse where there are some small waterfalls. You may be lucky to see a dipper here. There are some stone enclosures that are hafodydd or sheep pens. Eventually you meet an obvious track that ascends the headwall of the valley. Continue (S) across flat open moorland until you meet a small path that is the Beacons Way.

The rocks here are very hard well-bedded quartz sandstones which are the Basal Grits of the Millstone Grit formation that were formed in the Carboniferous period.

Turn left (E) ascend the stony ridge ahead and then (N) to Godre Garreg Las. To the south is the Amman Valley. ▸ There isn't an obvious path to follow but make sure you keep to the highest ground to avoid crossing the boulder fields which are found closer to the crags. There are good views to the east of Fan Hir and Bannau Brycheiniog.

Towards the end of the ridge are two distinct large circular cairns, **Carnau'r Garreg Las**. Continue north to descend the ridge and then swing west, dropping down to the Sawdde stream below. Pick a route that avoids boggy areas as much as possible and which brings you above the hill fence. Cross the stream as soon as possible and follow the bank down stream. ▸ When the stream becomes difficult to follow, climb up to the left and back onto the bridleway and retrace the route to the start.

This area is attractive with gnarled hawthorn trees dotted along the valley.

Woodland flowers in Cwm Cumbeth

7 THE BLACK MOUNTAINS (Y MYNYDDOEDD DUON)

WALK 40

Pen Cerrig-calch and Table Mountain

Start	Great Oak Road north of Crickhowell (SN691 141)
Map required	Eastern Map OL13
Distance	8.2km (5.1 miles); with extension 19.4km (12.1 miles)
Total ascent	568m (1862ft); with extension 1862m (3080ft)

This is one of the best of the Black Mountains high walks and has the added bonus of following 1.5km of Cwm Cumbeth, a wooded valley that is full of wildlife interest at its beginning. The summit of Pen Cerrig-calch is reached via Darren and this avoids the well-used ascent route via Table Mountain.

Start opposite an electricity sub-station on the Great Oak Road north of Crickhowell. Opposite this is a farm with a 'Private Road' sign and a yellow waymark. Take this to **The Wern** farm where you turn left in the yard. Table Mountain is ahead just on the right. Go through the gate and straight on with the hedge on your left, ignoring the footpath on the right, and cross over a stile. Continue straight across the field to the corner of the hedge. Follow the arrow on the post to a stile and on to a path between hedges to meet the path that runs along **Cumbeth Brook**. Here you join the Beacons Way and follow the path upstream.

The route is bordered by lesser celandine (yellow flower) and the woodland on the left has a tapestry of bluebells, dog violets, wood sorrel and wood anemones in the spring. The latter are often an indication of ancient woodland and a mixture of beech, oak, ash, hazel and holly can be seen. A variety of woodland birds (including tit, pied flycatcher, nuthatch, redstart, tawny owl and woodpecker, treecreeper) and butterflies can be found here.

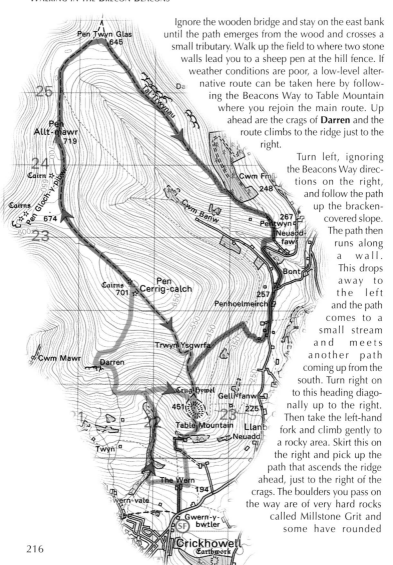

Ignore the wooden bridge and stay on the east bank until the path emerges from the wood and crosses a small tributary. Walk up the field to where two stone walls lead you to a sheep pen at the hill fence. If weather conditions are poor, a low-level alternative route can be taken here by following the Beacons Way to Table Mountain where you rejoin the main route. Up ahead are the crags of **Darren** and the route climbs to the ridge just to the right.

Turn left, ignoring the Beacons Way directions on the right, and follow the path up the bracken-covered slope. The path then runs along a wall. This drops away to the left and the path comes to a small stream and meets another path coming up from the south. Turn right on to this heading diagonally up to the right. Then take the left-hand fork and climb gently to a rocky area. Skirt this on the right and pick up the path that ascends the ridge ahead, just to the right of the crags. The boulders you pass on the way are of very hard rocks called Millstone Grit and some have rounded

The Brecon Beacons from Pen Cerrig-calch

white pebbles. These are composed of quartz conglomerate (see 'Geology of the Brecon Beacons,' Introduction).

To continue on the main route from Darren, follow a sheep track along the head of the valley and strike up to the summit of **Pen Cerrig-calch**. The summit itself is of Millstone Grit but just below this is a band of Carboniferous limestone which was once part of the Llangattock escarpment before the Usk Valley was formed. This is the only occurrence of limestone in the Black Mountains. Quartz conglomerates of the Plateau Beds are found below and then Brownstones and Senni Beds on lower ground. There is a selection of upland birds living here including skylarks, meadow pipits, stonechats and ravens (see 'Birds of the Mountains,' Walk 22).

The extended route to Pen Allt-mawr and Pen Twyn Glas leaves from here. To continue on the main route descend the path south-east from the summit, clamber down the steep section at **Trwyn Ysgwrfa** and climb the steps through the earth and stone ditches and ramparts onto **Table Mountain**.

Formed of the dip slope of the resistant Plateau Beds, Table Mountain is the impressive setting for Crug Hywel, an Iron Age **hill fort** that is thought to have been owned by Hywel Dda in the 10th century, a well-respected prince of South Wales. He was the grandson of Rhodri the Great, famous for killing the leader of the Viking invaders at Anglesey. Hywel introduced the Law of Wales, a set of social rules to free the common man from oppression by the upper classes.

Continue southwards down the dipping flat summit, keeping to the right-hand edge above the crags and descend the steps at the end. Drop down to the path below on the right and to the hill fence where the two dry-stone walls meet. Cross the stile and follow the path which then turns to the left and drops down the slope through a number of fields. Turn right to The Wern farm, ignoring the route which goes straight on to a stile. Turn left in the farmyard and retrace your steps to the start.

Extension
Continue north along the ridge and drop down slightly to a col. The path becomes stony and exposed with high winds and leads to the summit of **Pen Allt-Mawr** where there is a trig point. Descend north from the summit to **Pen Twyn Glas** at the head of Cwm Banw Valley. Keep below the crest of the ridge on your right and merge with a path descending **Tal Trwynau** ridge on your right.

The summit of Pen Twyn Glas (645m) is marked by two upright inscribed stones, which are 19th-century boundary markers bearing the names of local landowners, Mrs Macnamara 1811 and Sir J. Bailey Bart 1847, whose estates met at this point.

Arrive at a tall cairn and then to a forestry plantation followed by a gate and stile. Follow the forestry until it bears to the left where you continue down to a farm track. This eventually turns sharp left. At this point take the right of two gates and walk ahead for 50m and then left down the field at a waymarker. At the bridge, cross the river and walk up the road ahead for about 1.5 miles to **Green Cottage** on the right

Cairn on Tal Trwynau

where you join the Beacons Way. The track to the left of the cottage bears right along a wall to the ruins of Graig-lwyd. Continue up the hill past holly bushes and meet the path contouring around the lower slopes of Pen Cerrig-calch. Turn right and shortly left to meet a junction of paths. Take the left path climbing slowly upwards, taking the higher path where it divides to the col, with Table Mountain on the left, where you rejoin the main route.

WALK 41
Craig y Cilau and Cwm Onneu Fach

Start	Bend on minor road near Llangattock (SO206 169)
Map required	Eastern Map OL13
Distance	6.6km (4.1 miles)
Total ascent	187m (614ft)

A short walk that visits Craig y Cilau National Nature Reserve, which is designated for its rich limestone flora and is one of the National Park's treasures. Unusual trees are found here, including a species of whitebeam that is found nowhere else. The area was once a quarry and is now a caver's paradise with an entrance to the famous Ogof Agen Allwedd system.

Start at the sharp bend in the road just south-west of the bridge across the Monmouthshire and Brecon Canal. Cross the stile and follow the rather muddy path on the left through a gate and ignore the stile on the left. Pass a waymark post on the right and continue straight ahead where the track narrows to a path. Go through a gate, after which the path widens, passing behind **Cwm Bach** farm and holiday let cottages.

The track ahead crosses a small stream to a stile. Ahead is an obvious steep slope which was once a quarry incline. A climb of 250m brings you to an open area. There is a welcome wooden seat here with excellent views over to Table Mountain and Pen Cerrig-calch (Walk 40) on the far side of the valley beyond Crickhowell.

Take the path up behind the seat (SE). This steep path brings you to a grassy terrace running below the limestone crags. The Sugar Loaf Mountain is over to the east (Walk 42). Turn right, west, along the terrace to the National Nature Reserve information board.

Craig y Cilau was designated a National Nature Reserve in 1959 and it contains several caves, a rich flora and a number of uncommon trees, including several species of whitebeam. The short limestone cliffs were once quarried but now contain some of the finest limestone vegetation in the National Park.

The varied habitat from the scrub woodland on the lower slopes, up through the short limestone grassland

and sparsley wooded cliffs to the open moorland of the summit makes this an excellent reserve for many different insects and birds. Around 40 bird species have been recorded here, including ring ouzel, a migrant thrush that resembles a blackbird with a white bib. Clinging to the ledges of the cliffs, out of reach of grazing sheep, there are five notable species of whitebeam, one of which is unique to this locality. In the shaded woody area on the lower slopes another rarity in this area is the alpine enchanter's nightshade, here at the southern limit of its distribution in Britain.

Above the limestone escarpment is a capping of Millstone Grit and below the limestone are the sandstones, silts and clays of the Old Red Sandstone formation. The reserve therefore enjoys a very wide range of soil types which are reflected in the huge variety of flowering plants.

Continue round the terrace in a long sweeping arc (W and N). On a clear day the views and situation are remarkable. After the hollow of **Eglws Faen**, extensive limestone cliffs are

Craig y Cilau National Nature Reserve

221

reached and a waymarked path descends on the right into the valley. Leave this for the moment and continue to the end of the terrace to see **Agen Allwedd cave** entrance. The limestone itself is peppered with caves and Mynydd Llangattock contains extensive cave systems, including Ogof Agen Allwedd (37.5 km), Ogof Darren Cilau and Eglwys Faen. Agen Allwedd is an important winter roost for lesser horseshoe bats as well as having a colony of long-eared bats.

Backtrack to the waymarked path and descend gently to the valley. On the way down there is a fine view north past the high summits of Pen Cerrig-calch and Pen Allt-mawr to Pen Tir and Mynydd Troed. Castell Dinas can be seen in the far distance to the right of Mynydd Troed (Walk 45) and Waun Fach, the highest point in the Black Mountains, is just visible to the east.

The path branches at a waymarked post. Follow the yellow arrow down to the right between bracken and hawthorn trees. At the valley base turn left and continue up the valley, climbing slightly alongside a moss-covered wall on the right. At the sharp right bend in the wall continue straight ahead and into an interesting high bog, **Waun Ddu**. Small areas

The Sugar Loaf and Craig y Cilau

have been fenced off for experimental purposes and these harbour rushes and heathers. Continue onwards to another National Nature Reserve sign and beyond this to a stile and gate.

Cross this in an easterly direction to a sheep holding pen which you leave on the right via a stile. Follow the wall down to a gate and stile on the left. Aim for a large ash tree and stile. A path crosses the middle of the field ahead above the stream bed down to the right where three sheep gates allow you to cross the fence. The path continues along the wood on your left, arriving at a stile and a crossing of the stream. Ignore this and continue ahead, rising through the wood and to a large collapsed beech tree. Just past this drop down right to a gate into a field. Follow this route down the track leading up from the holiday cottages and retrace your steps to the start.

WALK 42

Crug Mawr and Sugar Loaf

Start	Red Lion Pub, Llanbedr (SO240 204)
Map required	Eastern Map OL13
Distance	21.6km (13.4 miles)
Total ascent	1216m (3990ft)

This is an all-day walk full of variety and interest, having two upland sections linked by tranquil wooded river valleys and two excellent pubs along the way. The highlight is a visit to the extraordinary Partrishow Church, which has a wealth of history spanning a thousand years. The return route climbs the Sugar Loaf and then drops down to Llangenny and a well-earned break at the Dragon's Head pub. A relaxing river walk brings you back to the start.

Start at the Red Lion pub in the village of Llanbedr. With the pub and church in front of you, take the track with a 'No-through road' sign on the right, which then swings around the edge of the graveyard and down to the river, the **Grwyne Fechan**, in the valley below. Cross Upper Cwm Bridge and take the stile on the left and follow the zigzag path up the valley side. The bridleway on your right is your return route. The path divides halfway up the slope. Take the left-hand fork.

The woodland is a mixture of ash, beech, sycamore and hazel and is particularly impressive in April and May when the understorey is carpeted with a mixture of lesser

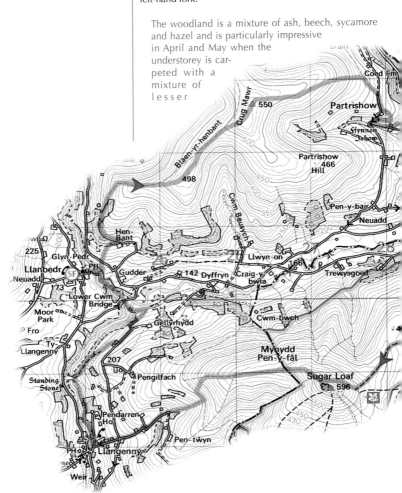

celandine (yellow flower), wood sorrel (delicate white flower), wood anemones (white flower), dog-violets and bluebells.

Cross the stile where the woodland finishes and into a field. Keep the fence on your left and this brings you to the road. There are excellent views to your right of the north slope of the Sugar Loaf which is on the return route. On your left is the Grwyne Fechan Valley with Table Mountain and Pen Cerrigcalch. Cross the road and the stile into a field. There is a break in the line of trees ahead and the route crosses an upright rock slab and a stile in the hedge just before this on your right. Head across the field to the left of the house to the start of a track. Shortly afterwards, take the bridleway on the left with a mossy dry-stone wall. ▶

Ignore the track that leaves on the right just before the woodland finishes and carry on to the gate where you turn right along the Beacons Way. Ahead are excellent views of the Grwyne Fechan Valley and up to the summits of Waun Fach and Pen y Gadair Fawr. Follow the path which runs alongside the dry-stone wall and ignore a gate in this. At a junction take the right-hand fork to the summit of **Blaen-yr-Henbant** where you can follow a sheep track along its left-hand edge along the top of a line of crags. The area here is covered in bilberry and the songs of skylarks can be heard in spring and summer (see 'Birdlife,' Introduction). A closer inspection of the Old Red Sandstone rocks shows they are red in colour and well-bedded (see 'Geology of the Brecon Beacons,' Introduction).

Drop down to a col with Cwm Beusych to your right and Cwm Milaid to your left. The Beacons Way skirts below the

Grwyne Fechan and Table Mountain

The woodland here has a superb carpet of bluebells in the spring.

225

summit of **Crug Mawr** but take the small path that leads to the trig point. The area is covered with heather and bilberry and has excellent panoramic views. On a clear day it is possible to see the Cotswolds and the Malvern Hills to the east and the Severn Estuary to the south.

From the trig point, descend east along a path passing a small pond to where it runs alongside the hill fence to a gate marked 'Beacons Way'. Follow this down to the road and continue straight ahead to where a footpath signposted to Ty'n-y-llwyn leaves on a bend just before a stone barn. Take this and cross the field and then turn right along a break in the slope before you reach the farm to **Partrishow Church**.

Partrishow Church was established in the mid-11th century and has a rare surviving medieval rood screen and loft which date back to c1500. The church is entered through a 14th-century porch and houses a splendidly carved oak rood screen from the late 15th century, two stone altars in front and a 16th-century chest hewn out of a single tree trunk The font at the rear is carved out of one block of stone and has an inscription of c1055,

Partrishow Church

making it one of the oldest in Wales. A number of old wall paintings were discovered during restoration in 1909, one of which is a chillingly eerie 'Doom Figure' which depicts a skeleton carrying a scythe, an hourglass and a spade and is reputedly painted with human blood. A 17th-century copy of the Ten Commandments is the clearest of the many other interesting wall paintings.

Carry on through the graveyard to the road, turn left and follow the road to the bend and **Ffynnon Ishow**.

Ffynnon Ishow is the secluded holy well of St Issui, an early Christian priest, who lived near the well and gave hospitality to pilgrims. Legend has it that a continental pilgrim was cured of leprosy here and left much gold to build the church. The approach to the well is indicated by a stone marked with a Maltese cross, which is thought to have been a mediaeval pilgrim's stone. Unfortunately, Issui met his death at the hands of an ungrateful traveller.

Take the footpath on the left just above the well. It crosses the field, with the church up to the left, and leads to the impressive house of **Tyn-y-llwyn**. Cross the stile and take the path on the left, marked 'Beacons Way' and follow this to the road. Cross this and down to the bridge over the **Grwyne Fawr** river and turn right on the tarmac road before Tabernacle Church. This becomes a footpath at **Ty-coch** where you continue straight ahead above a house, following the valley to **Pentwyn** and then to a T-junction with a road.

Turn right here and drop down to a five-way road junction. Continue straight ahead to Pontyspig in the direction of the Sugar Loaf. After about 100m, take the footpath on the left and head straight across the field to a stile and cross a small stream. Head for the stile in the opposite fence. Pass through woodland using boardwalks, cross a stile and head for the house across the field.

Turn left at the road and first right to a junction where you bear left. Continue to a large oak tree on the right that marks where the path leaves for the Sugar Loaf 3.2km away. Take this and shortly after cross the stile in the hill fence where there is a National Trust sign. Carry straight on, ignoring the path on the right. The path runs along a fence with trees on the left and then cuts up the hill through bracken that changes to heather and bilberry. It follows a stone wall then leaves this where the wall turns left.

Take the right-hand fork heading for the summit. This meets a path coming up from the left. Bear right at this point and take the path, an old quarry track, that works its way around the northern side of the summit and eventually to the top of **Sugar Loaf**.

The great effort is rewarded with superb panoramic views. Due east is the steep slope of the Ysgyryd Fawr, north-west is Pen Cerrig-calch and west in the distance are Pen y Fan and Corn Du, the highest summits in South Wales. On a clear day it is possible to look south over Abergavenny and to the Severn Estuary and the Devon hills beyond. The Grwyne Fawr Valley below to the north formed as a result of major geological fault in the earth's crust called the Neath Disturbance (see 'Earth Movements,' Introduction).

Head (W) down the path across **Mynydd Pen-y-fal**. At the junction , take the right-hand fork with Llanbedr down to the right and then left when the path divides again and drops to the hill fence in the direction of **Llangenny**. Turn left and before the path starts to rise again there is a gate. Go through

Sugar Loaf from above Llangenny

228

this and follow the valley down to a track and then the road. Carry straight on to the bridge over the Grwyne Fawr river. The Dragon's Head pub is just on the other side.

Just before the bridge on the east bank is a stile and a footpath that runs upstream. ▶ The path comes to a stone bridge and this is where you have to leave the river bank. A yellow arrow directs you to turn right along a fence to a post with a 'Danger' warning sign. Turn left here along the obvious path to a stile and a narrow path. Cross over at the junction of the paths and to a stile. Shortly after, ignore the path that drops down to the left and continue to some cottages and the road.

Turn left and then left again when there is a 'Private Road' sign. Descend the track and take the first footpath on the left. The path drops down through the woodland to a bridge across the river and across a field to a road. Cross over this into a field with the river on your left. A path climbs up to a track where you turn left and continue following the river, ignoring the first bridge and continue to the bridge you crossed at the beginning of the walk. Turn left over the bridge and retrace your steps to the start.

The woodland has a great show of flowers in the spring.

WALK 43

Llanthony Priory, Offa's Dyke and Bal Mawr

Start	Llanthony Priory, Vale of Ewyas (SO288 278)
Map required	Eastern Map OL13
Distance	18.36km (11.4 miles)
Total ascent	929m (3048ft)

A classic route that takes in two ridges and the beautiful Vale of Ewyas. The walk starts at the impressive Llanthony Priory and climbs up to Offa's Dyke, the boundary between England and Wales. Other important religious buildings are discovered at Capel-y-ffin before another ascent to the ridge and on to Bal Mawr. The excellent pub at the priory is a welcome treat at the end of the day.

Start in front of **Llanthony Priory** where there is a sign marked 'Hill Walks' on the left. Take this to the northern side of the priory, follow the track marked 'Offa's Dyke North' and then the path marked 'All Routes' on your left to a gate. The path takes the western flank of Cwm Siarpal to the corner of Loxidge wood, crosses the hill fence and then climbs **Loxidge Tump** to **Offa's Dyke**. Offa's Dyke marks the border between Wales and England. The deep ditch and dyke structure was built in the eighth century by the Mercian ruler King Offa in an attempt to keep the Welsh out of his kingdom. The heather moorland here is important for rowan and merlin, with 2700 acres having been acquired by the National Park. It is managed as a grouse moor and has the largest breeding population in the National Park.

Look back for a superb view of Llanthony Priory.

Llanthony Priory was one of the earliest houses of Augustinian canons to be founded in Britain. The knight William de Lacy is said to have come across a ruined chapel of St David whilst out hunting. A church, dedicated to John the Baptist, was built on this site which was reorganised as a priory in about 1118. Giraldus Cambrensis visited in the 12th century and wrote of the priory as being 'fixed amongst barbarous people'. In 1135, the 40 canons were forced to retreat to Hereford and Gloucester and the building was destroyed. They were brought back by the de Lacy family and a great rebuilding phase between 1180 and 1230 resulted in the construction of the priory's church, one of the greatest medieval buildings in Wales.

Llanthony Priory and Bal Mawr

Turn left (NW) along the ridge to a 'mile post' to Red Daren down to the east. Continue along the peaty crest of the ridge where some of the wettest parts have been protected by large flagstones. Pass the trig point where there are good views down into the Crasswell and Llanvenoe Valleys and, in the foreground, the picturesque Olchon Valley. Turn left at another 'mile stone', taking the path south-west down a spur and picking up a stony path to the left towards Nant Vision. Follow the path that zigzags through bracken and then turns west along the hill fence to a stile after around 100m. The Honddu Valley is classic U-shape and was cut by a glacier during the last Ice Age.

Cross this and descend steeply through woodland to another style. Aim for the farm and follow a finger post right above the hedgerow to a stile and the lane to **Vision Farm**. Turn right up the valley, passing behind **Ty'r-onen Farm**, onto a wide unmade track to a ford. Cross this and a stile ahead and cross the field to the corner of the trees. Cross a small stream over a stone stile and continue to a second stone stile. Cross the field ahead to a sandy track and a gate behind **Blaenau Farm** leading to the yew tree encircled **St Mary's Church**. ◄

Measuring 8m by 4m, St Mary's church is one of the smallest in the country and was built in 1762.

St Mary's Church at Capel-y-ffin

Walk down to the main road crossing the river bridge and take the road on your right to the Grange Trekking Centre. Pass a tempting stone gateway and then take the narrow road on the left from where you can see the **old monastery**.

LLANTHONY TERTIA MONASTERY

The Anglican monastery of Llanthony Tertia was founded in 1870 by the eccentric Joseph Leycester Lyne who took the religious name of Father Ignatius. Lyne, an Anglican lay reader, was inspired by the monastic revival of the late 19th century and was determined to found an Anglican Benedictine religious order. There was a great deal of opposition to his ideas and he found it impossible to persuade any of the Anglican bishops to ordain him as a priest or to support him in any way. This was hardly surprising as the daily ritual was for the monks to take it in turns to be led into the cloister with a halter, to be spat on, walked over by the rest of the community and to beg for their bread.

Walk up to **The Grange Guest House** and turn left up a stony lane through a gate and follow a zigzag track up the hillside to the crest of the hill to a stone called the Blacksmith's Anvil. Down to the west is the glacially cut U-shaped Grwyne Fawr Valley. To the north is Lord Hereford's Knob on the left and Hay Bluff to the right. Below the reservoir is the Mynydd Du conifer plantation, a huge blight on the landscape, and beyond are the high summits of Pen Allt-mawr and Pen Cerrig-calch.

Continue (SE) along **Chwarel y Fan**, **Bwlch Bach** and **Bwlch Isaf** to the summit of **Bal Mawr**. The Sugar Loaf Mountain is over to the south-west and Ysgwrd Fawr to the south-east. Descend south-east from the trig point to meet a crossroads on the level ground at **Bal-Bach**. Turn left onto the Beacons Way and descend the path that leads into **Cwm Bwchel** and follows the stream course on its northern side. There are fine views of the priory in the valley below. Cross the hill fence just above the buildings and follow the way-mark signs for the Beacons Way down to the road and back to the start at the priory.

WALK 44
Lord Hereford's Knob and Nant Bwch

Start	Bridge over the Afon Honddu, Capel-y-ffin (SO255 315)
Map required	Eastern Map OL13
Distance	10.5km (6.5 miles)
Total ascent	363m (1191 ft)

An excellent route that explores a picturesque and surprisingly remote side valley of the Vale of Ewyas. A steep initial ascent is followed by a ridge walk to Lord Hereford's Knob from where there are fine panoramic views of Mid-Wales to the north-west and of the glacial U-shaped valley of the River Honddu. There is plenty of historical interest with two churches and a monastery.

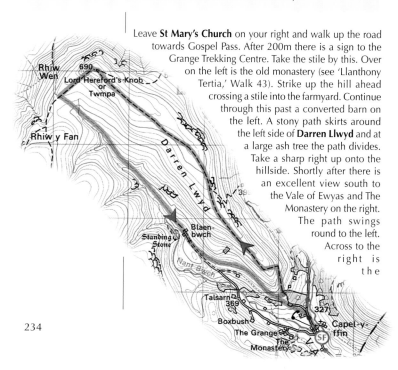

Leave **St Mary's Church** on your right and walk up the road towards Gospel Pass. After 200m there is a sign to the Grange Trekking Centre. Take the stile by this. Over on the left is the old monastery (see 'Llanthony Tertia,' Walk 43). Strike up the hill ahead crossing a stile into the farmyard. Continue through this past a converted barn on the left. A stony path skirts around the left side of **Darren Llwyd** and at a large ash tree the path divides. Take a sharp right up onto the hillside. Shortly after there is an excellent view south to the Vale of Ewyas and The Monastery on the right. The path swings round to the left. Across to the right is the

Nant Bwch from Lord Hereford's Knob

hill ridge carrying Offa's Dyke, which forms the boundary between Wales and England.

At the divide in the path take the left-hand climbing path which shortly doubles back (SW) and onto the prow of the hill. Turn right (N) and soon reach a well-built shelter below the summit. Continue north to a true cairn still below the summit. Continue climbing gently and the path becomes alternately sandy and muddy between heather. At the fork, take the right path and continue gently to the badly eroded summit area with first a collapsed cairn and then a standing cairn. There is a small cairn on the summit of **Lord Hereford's Knob**, also known as the Twmpa.

Descend south-west from the summit. On a clear day the Brecon Beacons can be seen straight ahead. At the lowest point on the escarpment a track descends steeply (N) into the valley. At this point take the bridleway (SE), soon picking up a small stream, the start of **Nant Bwch**. Make sure to descend on its left bank into a quickly steepening valley. There are small waterfalls in a side valley joining from the west. The path remains well above the river and follows a man-made ledge, presumably a quarry route.

The path drops down the valley and fords a small stream joining from the east where there is a fine waterfall and stone

235

refuge. Continue to **Blaen-Bwch Farm**. Leave the road on a footpath on the left opposite the first stand of trees on the hillside above. This soon joins the bridleway that contours around the hillside to where the hill fence was crossed earlier. Retrace your steps to the start.

WALK 45
Castell Dinas and Waun Fach

Start	Castle Inn, Pengenffordd, A479 Talgarth to Tretower (SO174 296)
Map required	Eastern Map OL13
Distance	14.6km (9.1 miles)
Total ascent	510m (1673ft)

A superb walk that ascends Waun Fach, the highest mountain in the Black Mountains, and has stunning panoramic views. The descent comes down Y Grib, a narrow spur of land, to Castell Dinas, an impressive Iron Age hill fort with a commanding view of the Rhiangoll Valley.

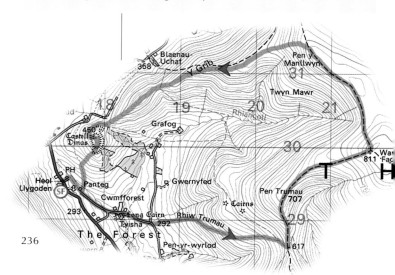

At the northern end of the pub car park, descend a set of wooden steps marked with a waymark arrow to Castell Dinas into the lane below and turn right down the track. After about 50m there is a stile on the left. Ignore this – it will be your descent route at the end of the walk. Walk behind and below the Castle Inn and after 200m the track divides. Keep to the left past a farm and cross a ford to meet a road on a bend. Turn left and follow the road to where another road joins from the left.

Shortly afterwards, turn left onto a bridleway to the hill fence. The lower slopes of mountains ahead are formed of the Senni Beds with the summits composed of the more resistant Brownstones (see 'Geology of the Brecon Beacons,' Introduction). Cross **Rhiw Trumau** to the cairn at the col. Turn north and follow the ridge along **Pen Trumau** to **Waun Fach.** Far to the east, the Shropshire Clee Hills are visible and to the south you may glimpse the Bristol Channel. To the west are the Brecon Beacons and the Carmarthen Fans. ▶

Listen out for skylarks singing in the spring and summer.

Take the obvious path that descends a little to the north and then skirts around the eastern ridge of the Rhiangoll Valley. Climb slightly to **Pen y Manllwyn** and about 500m from the rather unclear summit drop down the hillside in a westerly direction to the **Y Grib**. Keep to the summit of the ridge, avoiding the paths to right and left which descend below the ridge itself. There are three sections to the ridge

The view south from Y Grib of the Rhiangoll Valley

237

Y Grib and Lord Hereford's Knob from Castell Dinas

with short descents and climbs to the separate summits, and a substantial cairn is passed on the way down past a few rocky outcrops. On the last summit before the castle hill is a round stone shelter.

Drop down quite steeply from this to a gate ahead. Cross the stile and climb up ahead to the remains of **Castell Dinas**. A more obvious path to the right should be avoided as it bypasses the castle remains.

> Castell Dinas is an Iron Age hill fort whose ramparts, steep sides and great ditches are still well defined. It is hard to believe that these were probably built as early as 500BC. A Norman motte and bailey style castle was also built on the site but there is little remaining of this stone stronghold.

Drop down to the right, leaving the small coniferous plantation on your left, to a stile. Descend the field, keeping the fence to your right, to reach another stile. Keep descending to the stream, which is easily crossed to a stile leading into the lane where the walk began. Turn right for 50m to the steps and back to the start.

APPENDIX 1
Routes by Difficulty

Walk	Start	Distance	Total ascent	Steepness of ascents and descents	Exertion	Route finding	Suitability in bad weather
1	Llwynbedw, Cwm Llwch	9.5km (6 miles)	620m (2035ft)	4	4	3	N
2	Llwynbedw, Cwm Llwch	10km (6 miles)	620m (2035ft)	4	4	3	N
3	Llwynbedw, Cwm Llwch	6km (3.75 miles)	340m (1115ft)	1	2	1	Y
4	Pont y Caniedydd	9.5km (6 miles)	560m (1841ft)	4	4	3	N
5	Pont y Caniedydd	11km (6.5 miles)	641m (2103ft)	4	4	3	N
6	Pont y Caniedydd	10km (6 miles)	560m (1841ft)	5	4/5	3	N
7	Pont y Caniedydd	6.25km (3.6 miles)	250m (820ft)	1	2	1	Y
8	Pont y Caniedydd	8km (5 miles)	641m (2102ft)	4	3	3	N
9	Pen-yr-heol	8.75km (5.2 miles)	410m (1350ft)	3	3	3	N
10	Pen-yr-heol	8km (5 miles)	605m (1985ft)	4	4	3	N
11	Pont y Caniedydd	8.75km (5.6 miles)	350m (1150ft)	1	2	1	Y
12	Pen-yr-heol	9.75km (6 miles)	436m (1430ft)	4	4	4	N
13	Near Tregaer Farm, Llanfrynach	13.75km (8.4 miles)	540m (1818ft)	4	4	2	N

Walk	Start	Distance	Total ascent	Steepness of ascents and descents	Exertion	Route finding	Suitability in bad weather
14	Near Tregaer Farm, Llanfrynach	15km (9.3 miles)	566m (1857ft)	2	4	4	N
15	Near Tregaer Farm, Llanfrynach	5km (3.2 miles)	200m (328ft)	1	1	2	Y
16	Pencelli Church	6.25km (3.6 miles)	386m (1266ft)	2	2	2	Y
17	Talybont Reservoir car park	7.5km (5 miles)	570m (1850ft)	3	4	3	N
18	Pont Blaen-y-glyn Forestry Commission car park	9.25km (6 miles)	490m (1607ft)	2	3	2	Y
19	Pont Blaen-y-glyn Forestry Commission car park	10km (6 miles)	490m (1608ft)	2	3	2	Y
20	Torpantau Forestry Commission car park	13km (8.5 miles)	354m (1160ft)	3	4	3	N
21	Taf Fechan Forestry Commission car park	12.5km (7.6 miles)	650m (2132ft)	3	4	2	N
22	Pont Nant Gwinau (A470)	8.75km (5.2 miles)	220m (720ft)	2	3	4	N
23	Forestry Commission plantation near Nant Crew Bridge (A470)	7.5km (4.8 miles)	420m (1500ft)	3	3	3	N

Walk	Start	Distance	Total ascent	Steepness of ascents and descents	Exertion	Route finding	Suitability in bad weather
24	A470 N of Storey Arms Centre	3.3km (2 miles)	280m (918ft)	3	1	1	Y
25	Nant-yr-Eira Bridge	9km (5.6 miles)	350m (947ft)	1	2	4	N
26	Near Forest Lodge Cottages	7.5km (5 miles)	270m (886ft)	1	2	3	Y
27	Sarn Helen	16.25km (10.4 miles)	212m (696ft)	1	4	3	N
28	South of Maen Llia	10km (6.4 miles)	442m (1450ft)	1	2	3	N
29	Pontneddfechan	8km (5 miles)	–	1	1	1	Y
30	Pontneddfechan	18km (11.2 miles)	–	2	4	2	Y
31	Penderyn	10km (6 miles)	–	2	3	2	Y
32	Coed y Rhaiadr Forestry Commission car park	14km (8.7 miles)	–	2	3	2	Y
33	Pont Mellin-fach car park	13km (8 miles)	–	1	3	2	Y
34	Head of the Sawdde Valley	14km (8.75 miles)	637m (2089ft)	4	3	3	N
35	Llandeilo Road bridge, near Glanaman	5.6km (3.5 miles)	263m (2089ft)	1	2	2	Y

Walk	Start	Distance	Total ascent	Steepness of ascents and descents	Exertion	Route finding	Suitability in bad weather
36	Pont Haffes	20.5km (12.7 miles)	744m (2415ft)	3	5	5	N
37	Cwm Twrch Uchaf	14.7km (9.2 miles)	496m (1628ft)	2	4	4	N
38	Ynyswen (A4067)	7km (4.4 miles)	122m (400ft)	1	1	1	Y
39	Pont Aber (A4069)	14km (8.6 miles)	495m (1624ft)				
40	Great Oak Road north of Crickhowell	8.2km (5.1 miles) extension 19.4km (12.1 miles)	568m (1862ft); with extension 1862m (3080ft)	3	3/5	3	N
41	Near Llangattock	6.6km (4.1 miles)	187m (614ft)	1	1	1	Y
42	Llanbedr	21.6km (13.4 miles)	1216m (3990ft)	2	5	2	N
43	Llanthony Priory	18.36km (11.4 miles)	929m (3048ft)	2	5	2	N
44	Capel-y-ffin	10.5km (6.5 miles)	363m (1191 ft)	2	3	2	N
45	Pengenffordd	14.6km (9.1 miles)	510m (1673ft)	3	3	3	N

APPENDIX 2
Routes by Interest

Walk	Start	Geomorphology (glacial)	Geology	Birds	Flowers	Waterfalls	Panoramas	Archaeology
1	Llwynbedw, Cwm Llwch	5	3	4	5	2	5	3
2	Llwynbedw, Cwm Llwch	4	3	3	5	0	5	3
3	Llwynbedw, Cwm Llwch	5	2	4	4	2	0	0
4	Pont y Caniedydd	5	4	3	4	0	5	4
5	Pont y Caniedydd	3	4	3	4	0	4	0
6	Pont y Caniedydd	5	4	2	4	0	4/5	4
7	Pont y Caniedydd	2	3	3	2	0	0	0
8	Pont y Caniedydd	3	3	4	3	0	4	1
9	Pen-yr-heol	3	2	4	2	0	4	1
10	Pen-yr-heol	4	3	3	2	0	4	1
11	Pont y Caniedydd	2	2	2	2	0	0	1
12	Pen-yr-heol	2	2	4	3	1	5	4

Walk	Start	Geomorphology (glacial)	Geology	Birds	Flowers	Waterfalls	Panoramas	Archaeology
13	Near Tregaer Farm, Llanfrynach	2	2	4	3	1	5	1
14	Near Tregaer Farm, Llanfrynach	2	2	3	2	0	5	1
15	Near Tregaer Farm, Llanfrynach	2	2	3	3	1	0	1
16	Pencelli Church	2	1	2	2	0	5	0
17	Talybont Reservoir car park	2	2	2	2	0	4	2
18	Pont Blaen-y-glyn Forestry Commission car park	3	3	4	3	3	5	0
19	Pont Blaen-y-glyn Forestry Commission car park	3	3	4	3	4	5	0
20	Torpantau Forestry Commission car park	3	3	3	2	1	5	1
21	Taf Fechan Forestry Commission car park	4	3	3	3	0	5	3

Walk	Start	Geomorphology (glacial)	Geology	Birds	Flowers	Waterfalls	Panoramas	Archaeology
22	Pont Nant Gwinau (A470)	2	2	2	2	1	2	0
23	Forestry Commission plantation near Nant Crew Bridge (A470)	3	3	2	2	1	3	0
24	A470 N of Storey Arms Centre	4	3	5	5	0	2	1
25	Nant-yr-Eira Bridge	3	2	2	2	0	4	0
26	Near Forest Lodge Cottages	3	3	5	5	0	3	3
27	Sarn Helen	4	3	5	5	0	3	3
28	South of Maen Llia	2	2	1	2	0	5	2
29	Pontneddfechan	2	4	4	4	5	0	5
30	Pontneddfechan	2	5	5	4	5	0	5
31	Penderyn	5	5	5	4	5	2	5
32	Coed y Rhaiadr Forestry Commission car park	5	5	5	4	5	0	5
33	Pont Mellin-fach car park	5	5	5	5	5	0	2

Walk	Start	Geomorphology (glacial)	Geology	Birds	Flowers	Waterfalls	Panoramas	Archaeology
34	Head of the Sawdde Valley	5	3	3	2	0	5	3
35	Llandeilo Road bridge, near Glanaman	1	2	5	3	0	3	0
36	Pont Haffes	5	4	2	2	0	5	3
37	Cwm Twrch Uchaf	2	5	4	3	3	4	5
38	Ynyswen (A4067)	1	5	5	4	5	2	0
Insert F6/39	Pont Aber (A4069)							
40	Great Oak Road north of Crickhowell	3	2	3	4	0	5	3
41	Near Llangattock	1	2	5	5	0	3	3
42	Llanbedr	2	2	4	4	0	5	5
43	Llanthony Priory	2	1	2	2	0	4	5
44	Capel-y-ffin	2	2	3	1	1	5	4
45	Pengenffordd	2	2	3	2	0	5	4

APPENDIX 3
Index of Information Boxes and Points of Interest

Information boxes are listed below in bold type and points of interest in Roman type.

APPENDIX 4
Brief Welsh–English Glossary

aber	river mouth	*cwar*	quarry
aderyn	bird	*cwm*	valley
afon	river	*cymmer*	meeting of rivers
allt	wooded	*ddinas*	fort
aran	high place	*dol*	meadow
bach	little or small	*drws*	door
ban, bannau	peak or crest	*du, ddu*	black
blaen	end, point, top, head of	*duwynt*	windy
bod	dwelling	*dwfr, dwr*	water
bont	bridge	*dyffryn*	valley
bryn	hill	*eglwys*	church
bwlch	pass	*eira*	snow
cadair	chair	*esgair*	ridge
cae	field	*fach*	peak
caer	fort, stronghold	*fan*	peak or crest
canol	middle	*fawr*	great or large
capel	chapel	*fechan*	smaller
carn/carnedd	cairn or heap	*felin*	mill
carreg	stone or rock	*ffordd*	road
castell	castle	*ffynon*	spring/well
cau	hollow	*foel*	rounded bare hill
cefn	ridge	*gallt*	wooded hill
celli	grove, copse	*garn/garnedd*	cairn/heap
cemaes	river bends	*garth*	hill
cerrig	stones	*glas*	blue/green
cilfach	corner, nook	*gleisiad*	young salmon
clawdd	hedge or ditch	*glyn*	valley
clog	crag, cliff	*goch*	red
clogwyn	cliff	*gwaun*	moor
clun	meadow	*gwladus*	white lady
clydach	torrent	*gwyn/gwen*	white
clyn-gwyn	white meadow	*gwynt*	wind
coch	red	*hafodydd*	summer dwellings
coed	wood	*hebog*	hawk
comin	common	*hen*	old
craig	rock/crag	*heol*	road
crib	combe/sharp ridge	*isaf*	lower
cribin	rocky ridge	*llan*	village/church
croes	crossroads	*llech*	flat stone/slate

llithrig	slippery
llwch	lake
llwyd	grey, brown
llyn	lake
maen	stone/block
maes	field/meadow
melin	mill
melyn	yellow
moel	rounded/bare hill
mynydd	mountain
nant	stream
neuadd	hall
newydd	new
ogof	cave
pant	hollow, valley
pentre	village, homestead
penyr	end of or top of
perfedd	middle
pistyll	spring, waterfall
plas	hall, mansion
pont	bridge
porth	gateway
pwll	pool
rhaidar	waterfall
rhiw	hill/slope
rhos	moorland
rhydd	ford
sarn	causeway, old road
sgwd	waterfall
sticill	stile
sych	dry
twll	hole
twyn	hill
uchaf	upper, highest
waun	moor
wen	white
y, yr	the
y groes	crossroads
y pannwr	the fuller
yr eira	snowy
ystrad	valley floor

APPENDIX 5
Useful Contacts

The **Brecon Beacons National Park** website (www.breconbeacons.org) is a great resource for things to do and see, transport, outdoor activities and where to stay.

Traveline Cymru (www.traveline-cymru.info) is a comprehensive interactive transport information site that will help you plan your best route to the Park. Abergavenny in the east is served by trains from Newport and Crewe while Llandeilo and Llandovery in the west are on the magical Heart of Wales line from Swansea. Merthyr Tydfil in the south has a direct connection to Cardiff. Train routes and timetables can be found at www.nationalrail.co.uk.

Coach travellers can reach Brecon via Cardiff and Abergavenny via Birmingham. **National Express** can be found at www.nationalexpress.com and **Stagecoach** at www.stagecoachbus.com. The **TrawsCambria network** (www.trawscambria.info) has a two hour service from Newtown/Llandrindod Wells (704) which connects with X43 in Brecon to Abergavenny or Merthyr Tydfil and Cardiff as well as the 714 to Llandovery.

The Park has a number of **information centres**:

- **National Park Visitor Centre** (Mountain Centre)
  at Libanus, six miles south of Brecon. Open all year. Tel: 01874 623366.

- **Craig-y-nos Country Park**
  in the upper Swansea Valley near Abercraf. Open all year. Tel: 01639 730395.

- **Abergavenny Tourist Information & National Park Centre**, Swan Meadow, Monmouth Road, Abergavenny NP7 5HL.
  Open Easter to October 9.30am–5.30pm; November to Easter 10am–4pm. Tel: 01873 853254.

- **Llandovery Tourist Information & Heritage Centre**, Town Centre, Llandovery SA20 0AW.
  Open November to Easter: 10am-1pm and 1.45–4pm Monday to Saturday; 11am–1pm Sunday. Tel: 01550 720693.

- **Waterfalls Centre**, Pontneathvaughan Road, Pontneddfechan, Nr Glynneath, SA11 5NR.
  Open April to October: 9.30am–1pm and 1.30pm–5.00pm, seven days a week. Tel: 01639 721795.

NOTES

LISTING OF CICERONE GUIDES

For full and up-to-date information
on our ever-expanding list of guides,
please visit our website:
www.cicerone.co.uk.

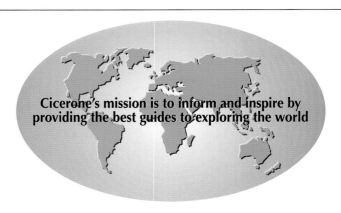

Cicerone's mission is to inform and inspire by providing the best guides to exploring the world

Since its foundation 40 years ago, Cicerone has specialised in publishing guidebooks and has built a reputation for quality and reliability. It now publishes nearly 300 guides to the major destinations for outdoor enthusiasts, including Europe, UK and the rest of the world.

Written by leading and committed specialists, Cicerone guides are recognised as the most authoritative. They are full of information, maps and illustrations so that the user can plan and complete a successful and safe trip or expedition – be it a long face climb, a walk over Lakeland fells, an alpine cycling tour, a Himalayan trek or a ramble in the countryside.

With a thorough introduction to assist planning, clear diagrams, maps and colour photographs to illustrate the terrain and route, and accurate and detailed text, Cicerone guides are designed for ease of use and access to the information.

If the facts on the ground change, or there is any aspect of a guide that you think we can improve, we are always delighted to hear from you.

Cicerone Press
2 Police Square Milnthorpe Cumbria LA7 7PY
Tel: 015395 62069 Fax: 015395 63417
info@cicerone.co.uk www.cicerone.co.uk